THE OCEAN EXPLORER'S DRAWING GUIDE FOR KIDS

Step-by-Step Lessons
for Observing and Drawing
Sea Creatures, Plants, and Birds

KRYSTAL AND BRAD WOODARD

of the

BRAVE KIDS
× ART CLUB ×

The Ocean Explorer's Drawing Guide for Kids:
Step-by-Step Lessons for Observing and Drawing Sea Creatures, Plants, and Birds

Krystal and Brad Woodard
Brave Kids Art Club

Editor: Kelly Reed
Project manager: Lisa Brazieal
Marketing coordinator: Katie Walker
Interior layout: Aren Straiger
Cover production: Aren Straiger
Cover artwork: Brad Woodard

ISBN: 979-8-88814-152-6
1st Edition (1st printing, July 2024)
© 2024 Brave the Woods
All images © Brad Woodard unless otherwise noted.

Rocky Nook Inc.
1010 B Street, Suite 350
San Rafael, CA 94901
USA

www.rockynook.com

Distributed in the UK and Europe by Publishers Group UK
Distributed in the U.S. and all other territories by Ingram Publisher Services

Library of Congress Control Number: 2023944106

This book is printed on acid-free paper.
Printed in China.

CONTENTS

About the
ILLUSTRATOR AND AUTHOR

Brad Woodard is a professional illustrator, teacher, and the host of Brave Kids Art Club online show and classes. Brad and his wife Krystal, the author of this book, grew up on separate sides of the country but both spent their time exploring and imagining the world around them. Their curiosity fueled their creativity, which only furthered their love for learning.

Brad and Krystal founded Brave Kids Art Club in hopes of offering a resource for kids to learn to be more confident, curious, and

talented artists and humans. Brave Kids Art Club is an online art education resource for kids, where Brad teaches kids that everybody can learn to draw and have a lot of fun doing it! Brad not only teaches basic drawing techniques, but also how to explore and learn about the fascinating world around us!

Brad and Krystal also run a creative agency called Brave the Woods, whose focus is making fun educational products for both kids, and those who are kids at heart. Brave the Woods has designed for major brands, children's books, animations, toys, and more!

BRAVE KIDS
⨯ ART CLUB ⨯

Find out more about Brave Kids Art Club at:

www.bravekidsartclub.com
www.bravethewoods.com

EXPLORING THE OCEAN

In order to draw the world around us, we need to experience the world around us!

Getting out into nature and exploring is the best way to observe nature. Bring your adventure backpack and take field notes everywhere you go.

When exploring the ocean, the best place to start is the beach! There are plants and animals everywhere if you know where to look. During low tide, many animals are left behind to observe in tidepools and can be found by carefully flipping over rocks and moving sand in the pools. Make sure to watch where you step as there is life everywhere in the tidepools.

Explorer Rules

✕ Always ask permission or take an adult with you.

✕ Don't touch animals you find, just observe them.

✕ Keep a safe distance from wild animals.

✕ Do not disturb or destroy an animal's habitat.

✕ If you catch an insect for observation, do not keep it for long. Release it where you found it.

Adventure Pack List

Pencil

Sketchbook

Eraser

Dark marker
or pen

Colors: Markers,
crayons, or
colored pencils

Bonus Gear:

Magnifying
glass

Binoculars

Camera

Bucket and
shovel

Scientists of the Ocean: Oceanographers and Marine Biologists

Oceanographers are scientists who study all aspects of the ocean, from the plants and animals to the seafloor and ocean water itself. They study the ecosystem of the ocean and all that it entails. Marine biologists specifically study the living creatures in the ocean. Both types of ocean scientists rely on observations and explorative questions. One of the best ways to record an observation is through drawing.

ASKING EXPLORATIVE QUESTIONS

The more you learn about what you are seeing, the better you will be able to draw it. To learn, you must ask questions. Asking explorative questions helps us understand why the thing we are observing is the way it is.

How do we ask explorative questions? First, we must gather information. These are some examples of exploratory questions:

What am I observing?

Is it living? Is it an animal, plant, or insect?

What makes it unique?

Is that unique aspect important?

How can I identify it?

Where did I find it?

What is its habitat?

By asking these kinds of questions, you are well on your way to being a scientist!

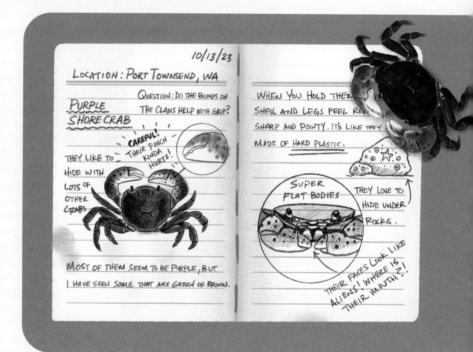

OCEAN EXPLORATION

Ancient civilizations began exploring the ocean by diving and building sailboats. They passed down what they learned through generations. As technology advanced, so did the methods for exploring the ocean. By the 1600s, the first submersibles were being designed and tested and in the 1700s diving suits were invented (though they were very heavy and looked different than what we use today).

With each invention came more of a desire to go deeper into the ocean and learn more. Technology today has made it possible for us to explore the oceans and discover new creatures that have never been discovered before. Despite the scientific advances and all humans have learned about the ocean in modern times, we still have not explored more than 80 percent of the ocean floor!

Ocean Health and Conservation

Over 70 percent of the Earth is ocean, which means the health of the ocean directly affects the health of the planet. We get food, resources to make medicines, and even jobs from the ocean. The ocean also plays a role in climate and weather. Unfortunately, through pollution and careless practices, ocean health is in danger.

Ocean conservation is actively helping protect the ocean and its ecosystems (all organisms living and interacting with each other in the ocean). Here are 5 ways you can help:

1 **Clean up the beach.** Whenever you are on the beach, pick up some trash. Trash can kill animals who get trapped in it or confuse it for food, and it pollutes the oceans.

2 **Use less plastics:** There are billions of pounds of plastics floating in the oceans. Using non-plastic items like reusable water bottles and bags, and recycling as much as possible, can help lessen the amount of plastics that end up in the ocean.

3 **Enjoy the ocean respectfully:** If boating, encourage adults to anchor away from coral reefs and sea grasses. Be careful to respect and not disturb the ocean habitats you find.

4 **Only use the water you need:** Conserve water by turning it off when you aren't using it, and remember that excess water drains to the ocean. Don't let the faucet run.

5 **Learn!** Learning more about the ocean and conservation is the best way to help! The more you know, the more you care. Speak up and teach others what you have learned so we can all work together to protect the ocean.

Drawing Techniques and Tips

BUILDING WITH SHAPES

Drawing things in nature can be difficult if you don't break down complex shapes into simple shapes first. You start by looking for basic shapes, build your form, and then add the details later. Going step-by-step makes the whole process much less intimidating.

Here are a couple drawing examples of building an animal with shapes.

Detailed harbor seal reference.

Look for basic shapes in animals.

Refine shapes while drawing.

Simplify hard shapes

TEXTURES AND PATTERNS: FUR, FEATHERS, SCALES

Remember: You don't always have to draw every single detail (but you can if you want). Even just a few feathers, tufts of fur, or a handful of scales gets the idea across without having to actually draw them all.

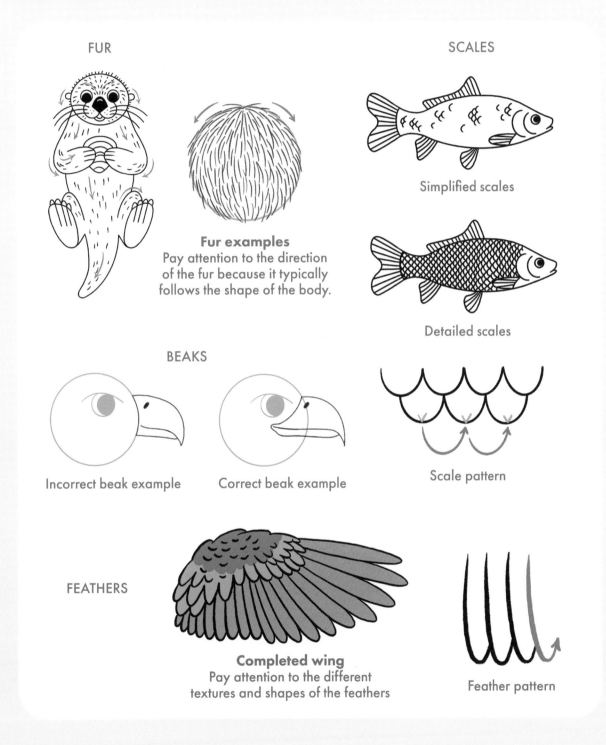

FUR

Fur examples
Pay attention to the direction of the fur because it typically follows the shape of the body.

SCALES

Simplified scales

Detailed scales

BEAKS

Incorrect beak example

Correct beak example

Scale pattern

FEATHERS

Completed wing
Pay attention to the different textures and shapes of the feathers

Feather pattern

FILLING IN OCEAN SCENES

The ocean is full of life. As you learn to draw your favorite ocean creatures, fill in the rest of your ocean scenes with some of these fun, simple drawings.

Next time you visit the beach, see how many of these you can find in the tide pools!

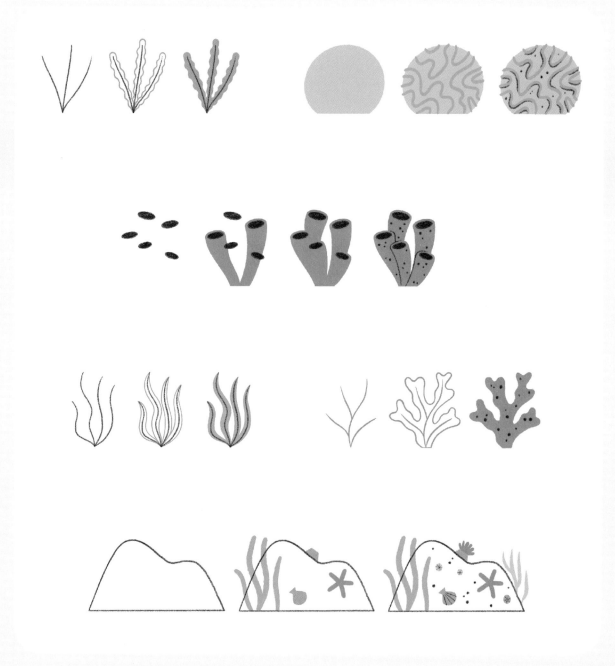

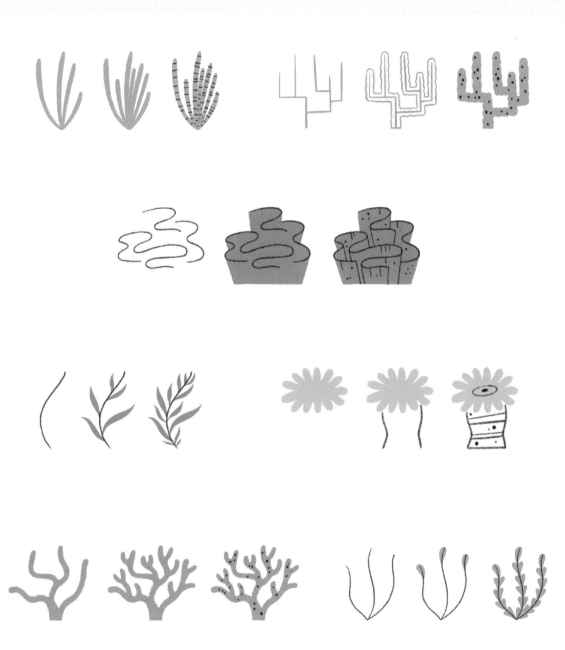

COLORING TIPS

Once you finish your drawing, it's time to color! You can mimic nature and make it accurate to your reference, or you can create something that has never been seen before. Have fun with it! Regardless of what you choose, here are a couple techniques to get you started.

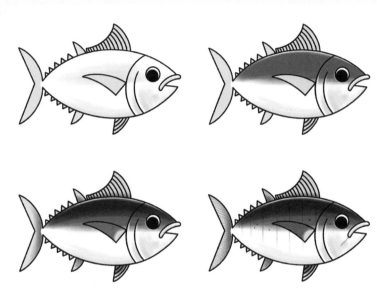

Color Layering

When coloring it is good to start with your lightest colors first, and then layer your darker colors on top. This can help you leave room for highlights and build up shadows to help your artwork look more dimensional.

Color Gradients

Example of color gradients

When you gradually transition, or blend, one color into another color, it is called a gradient. You can use two different colors, or use one color gradually applying less pressure to make it lighter and lighter. It's a great way to practice your blending and shading skills. Try it out!

Color Blending

The way you physically blend your colors depends on what type of coloring utensil you are using. If you are using tools like crayons or colored pencils, you blend colors by gradually applying more and more pressure as you overlap colors. The harder you press down the darker (opaque) your color will be, and vice versa. If you use markers, you can simply use color layering.

Analogous Colors

Whatever tools you use, a good rule for blending is to use colors next to each other on the color wheel, or analogous colors. They will blend very easily with one another if you pick one direction on the color wheel and follow it. Like this coral for example. Look at how the highlights are yellow and slowly we add oranges and eventually reds on the opposite side for the shadows.

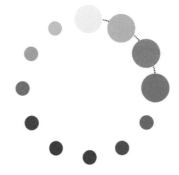

Color wheel example

Highlights and Shadows

Adding these will help your drawings have depth and dimension. Highlights are areas where light is shining directly. Shadows are areas that are blocked from the light. With that in mind, decide where your light is coming from and stick with that that entire time you are coloring.

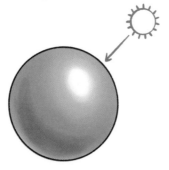

Look at this Tiger Barb fish. Can you tell where the light is coming from? Adding both highlights and shadows help it look less flat and more dimensional.

LET'S DRAW
GUIDE

Are you ready to draw? Great! Go grab your pencil and make sure you have an eraser handy—we are going to be doing a lot of erasing. Okay, let's get started!

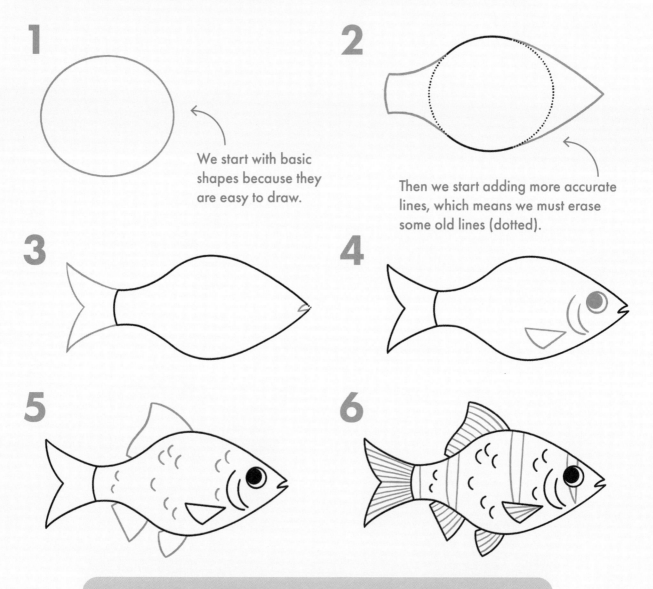

1 We start with basic shapes because they are easy to draw.

2 Then we start adding more accurate lines, which means we must erase some old lines (dotted).

3

4

5

6

TIP: Draw everything with a pencil first! Once you are happy with your sketch, you can outline it with a dark marker or pen to finalize it.

Final

Now color it in! If you want, you can copy these colors or you can choose your own. Use crayons, markers, paint, or whatever. Have fun!

KEY

• • • • • • • • • • • •   = Dotted lines are meant to be erased.

——————   = Black lines are what you already drew.

——————   = Orange lines are what you draw next.

Let's draw a...

CRAB

1

2

3

4

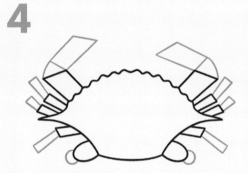

5

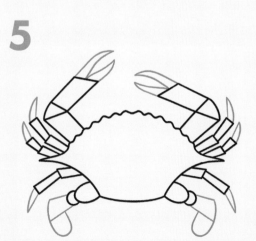

6

Crabs are decapod crustaceans, meaning they are animals with a hard protective shell and ten legs. The head and body are under their hard upper shell, or carapace. This shell is usually flat and rounded with serrated edges. Crabs have two pincers or claws at the end of their front legs.

OBSERVATIONS

Crabs are known for the large claws on their front legs. These strong pincers are used for catching prey, fighting, self-defense, and for tearing apart their food. They can regenerate claws that are broken off when they molt. Crabs also use their claws to communicate with each other by rubbing the ridges together to make noises.

Most crabs have ten legs, but the exact amount and what they are used for depends on the species. Many species have back paddle shaped legs for swimming called swimmerets. These special legs rotate quickly allowing the crab to swim. Crabs without swimmerets just walk around on the bottom of the ocean.

Crabs have complicated mouthparts that are made up of three parts: the mandible, maxillae, and maxillipeds. Mandibles crunch and grind the food. Maxillae "taste" the food and can detect chemicals, as well as separate food from sand. The maxillipeds are like another set of hands for the mouth to pass food into the mouth.

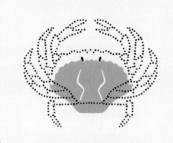

As crabs grow, they shed their old shell to make room for their new larger shell. When they do this, they must detach and push their body out of their old shell.

TIP:
Small crabs can often be found in tide pools on low tide, hiding under rocks and debris.

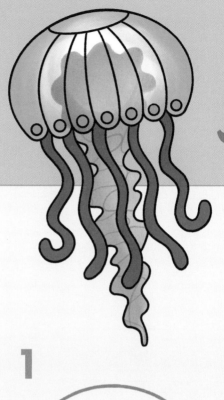

Let's draw a...

JELLYFISH

1

2

3

4

5

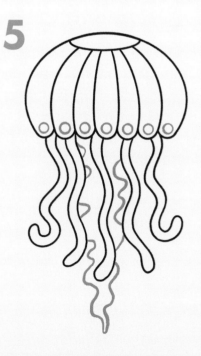

Jellyfish are part of the oldest animal groups on Earth, they have been around longer than the dinosaurs! Jellyfish have been floating around the ocean for over 650 million years. They have smooth bell-shaped bodies with stinging tentacles (anywhere from four to hundreds) and four long oral arms with a mouth in the middle.

OBSERVATIONS

Jelly fish are mostly made of water – they are 95 percent water to be exact. They have no heart, brain, bones, blood or even eyes so the remaining 5 percent of their bodies is made up of jelly-like layers containing nerve cells and their digestive system.

95%

Jellyfish eat fish, crustaceans (like crabs and shrimp), plankton, and sometimes even other jelly-fish. They have to digest their food very quickly so that it doesn't weigh them down, otherwise they wouldn't be able to float.

Some jellyfish are clear and completely see through. Other jellyfish can be a variety of vibrant colors such as pink, yellow, blue, or purple. About half of jellyfish are bioluminescent too, which means they glow in the dark!

TIP:
Dead jellyfish can still sting you so never touch a jellyfish, even if it is washed up on the beach. If you do get stung, have an adult help remove the tentacles, rinse with vinegar, and get medical help immediately.

Let's draw a...
PORTUGUESE MAN O' WAR

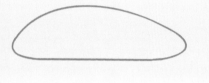

1

2

3

4

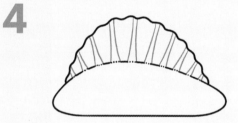

5

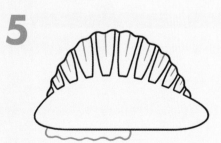

6

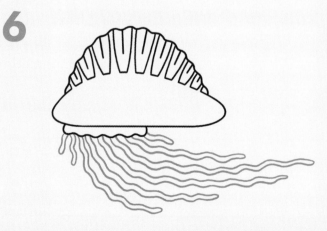

Portuguese Man o' War is a jellyfish-like creature called a siphonophore. Named after old Portuguese warships with open sails, the Portuguese Man o' War has what looks like a floating balloon with a mohawk on top. The float can range in color from clear to pink, blue, or purple. Under the float are the blue tentacles that extend below the surface.

OBSERVATIONS

Portuguese Man o' War are siphonophores, which means they are not one organism but instead a colony of organisms that survive together. These organisms are called zooids and they are actually identical clones of each other. There can be more than 1,000 zooids in each colony, and they all have a specific job to keep each other alive.

The colony of organisms that make up the Portuguese Man o' War include the pneumatophores (gas float), dactylozooids (tentacles for hunting and protection), gonozooids (polyp for reproducing), and gastrozooids (tentacles for eating and digesting).

The Portuguese Man o' War uses its tentacles and venom the same way as jellyfish, stinging its prey to capture and eat it. The tentacles can dangle up to 165 feet below the surface but average closer to 30 feet in length.

The float on top of the Portuguese Man o' War is how it moves. The float is filled with carbon monoxide and can be temporarily deflated if there is danger on the surface.

Tip:

Never touch a washed-up Portuguese Man o' War, even if it has been on the beach for a long time or is just an individual tentacle. They sting as a reflex and can inject venom when dead.

Let's draw a...

SEA ANEMONE

1

2

3

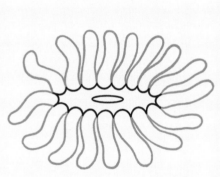

4

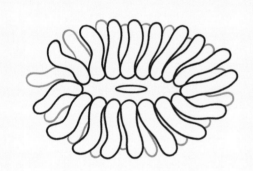

5

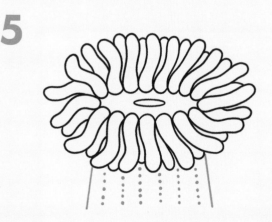

6

Sea anemone, named after anemone flowers, are the flowers of the sea. They are invertebrates, or boneless animals. They have a thick stalk with tentacles that come out of the top. The many bright colored tentacles surround a mouth called an oral disk.

OBSERVATIONS

Sea anemones spend most their lives stuck to rocks and coral with their foot at the bottom of the stalk. This foot, called a basal disc, adheres to a stationary object. They can still move though, and can walk by scooting their foot around, or swim by bending and twisting their bodies to move through the water.

Sea anemone tentacles sting using neurotoxins that paralyze their prey. When a fish, crab, or plankton come near, they quickly sting it and pull the prey into their mouth using their tentacles. Sea anemone only have one opening, which means they eat, and dispose of waste out of their mouth, which is called an oral disk.

Sea anemone tentacles range in colors from pinks, reds, purples, greens, white, and shades of yellow. Their color can depend on their natural pigment, how much sun they receive, and even from the algae on them and nutrients in the water. Sea anemones have a fluorescent protein that allows them to glow under UV light.

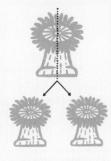

Sea anemone can reproduce in many ways. They can reproduce with another anemone, or they can also reproduce on their own. This is done by splitting themselves in half to make two separate anemones, or by creating small buds on their body that then pop off to be their own creatures.

BLUE WHALE

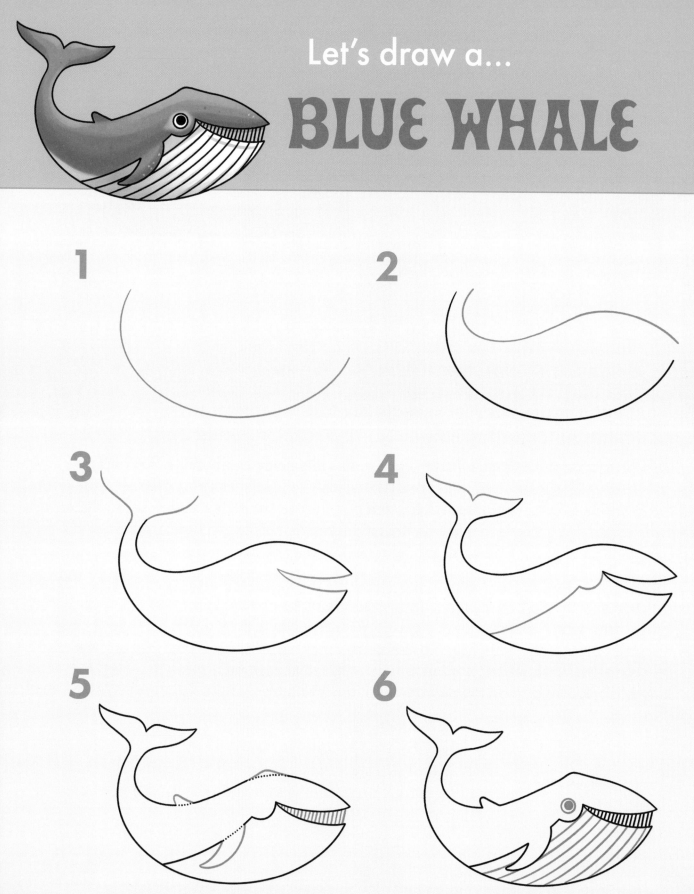

1

2

3

4

5

6

Blue whales are the largest animals on Earth. Their giant bodies are long and slender, reaching 80 to 100 feet in length. They have two long flippers, a relatively small dorsal fin, and wide thin flukes at the end of a thick tail stock. Blue Whales have a flat u-shaped head with a blow hole on top for breathing. They are a blotchy blue and gray color.

OBSERVATIONS

Blue whales are massive in every way. They are about the length of three school buses and the weight of 15 school buses. Their heart is the size of a car! Despite their huge size though, they eat tiny shrimp-like creatures called krill...but in massive amounts (up to 40 million krill a day).

Blue whales do not have teeth. To eat, they open their mouths wide and fill it with water, and then drain the water from their mouth through the bristly baleen plates hanging from their gums, trapping the krill inside.

Blue whales are the loudest animals on the planet. They use vocal sounds such as groans, moans, and sound pulses to communicate across the ocean, reaching up to 1,000 miles away. They make noises to communicate with their pods (families) and to locate food.

TIP:
According to surveys, only 1 percent of the world's population has seen a blue whale, so spotting one is a rare privilege.

Blue whales migrate thousands of miles seasonally to follow food sources and have their babies. They can be found traveling alone, or in small pods, and sometimes even in pods of up to 60 if there is a lot of krill in an area. Blue whales stay with their moms for about six months until they double in size.

Let's draw a...

DOLPHIN

1

2

3

4

5

6

Dolphins are sleek, streamlined mammals in the whale order ranging from four to 30 feet long. They have smooth rubbery skin that ranges from gray/blue to black on top and usually white on the bottom. They have two side flippers and a tall pointed dorsal fin on their back and a back tail or fluke. They have a long thin snout and blowhole on top of their head.

OBSERVATIONS

Dolphins' bodies are made for maneuvering quickly in the water and hunting. They typically cruise around 8 miles per hour but when hunting or trying to escape a predator, they can reach speeds of up to 25 miles per hour. They use their flexible fluke to propel them through the water and dive or change direction.

Dolphins are very social and live-in groups called pods that can be just a few dolphins to superpods that can be in the thousands. They work together in their pods to hunt and protect each other from predators. They even communicate with each other through clicks and whistles that make up their own language.

Dolphins are skilled hunters and use tools and tactics to make their lives easier. When dolphins hunt as a pod, they work together by kicking up dirt to confuse their prey or encircle fish and shrimp as a group to trap them in a small area. They have been seen using tools like sponges to protect their snouts when nosing around for food.

Dolphins have large brains and have the ability to problem solve, remember, reason, and understand. They are one of the few animals able to recognize themselves in a mirror. Scientists even believe that dolphin mothers give their babies names and that dolphins use those names to great each other throughout their lives.

Let's draw a...

GREAT WHITE SHARK

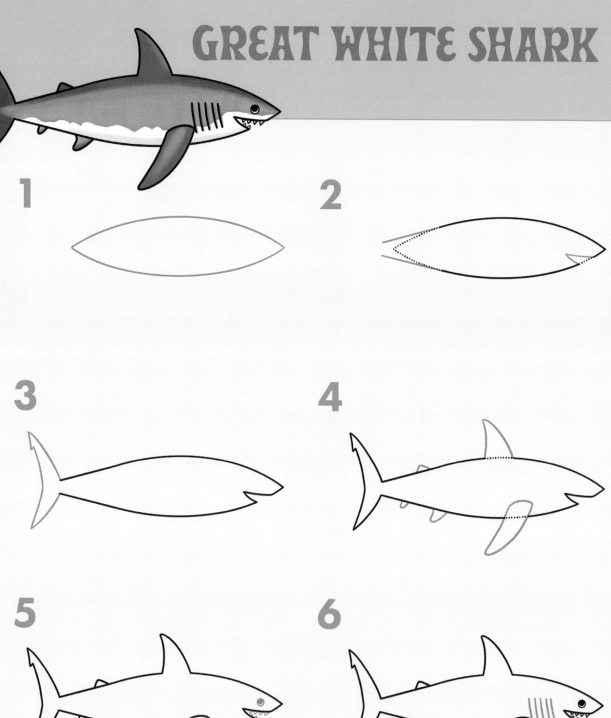

1

2

3

4

5

6

Great white sharks are large, torpedo-shaped fish with a pointed snout. They are not white like their name suggests, but instead gray to brown with a white belly. Great white sharks have two pectoral fins, a pelvic fin, an anal fin on their underside, and a small dorsal fin in addition to the signature pointed triangular dorsal fin on the top of their bodies and a large crescent shaped tail.

OBSERVATIONS

Great white sharks are the largest predatory fish on Earth and are apex predators, meaning nothing hunts them. Males are typically 11–13 feet long and females 15–16 feet long, but they can reach up to 20 feet long.

 Great white sharks have about 50 blade-like serrated teeth. Their upper jaw is loosely attached to their skulls, allowing them to push it forward and out of their mouth to take larger bites. Behind the first row of teeth are five or six more rows of teeth developing.

Great white sharks are skilled hunters and eat anything from fish, crustaceans, and rays to sea lions and even other sharks. They can sense electrical fields in water to find their prey. They use their camouflage backs to swim below their prey undetected.

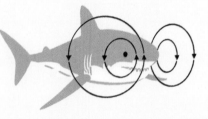

 Great white sharks are fast swimmers and travel at about 25 miles per hour. This is in part due to the dermal denticles covering their skin. Dermal denticles are tooth-like scales that interlock to give shark's skin a sandpaper texture and make them hydrodynamic. This feature helps them swim fast and quietly through the ocean.

TIP:
Great white sharks rarely attack humans and are more curious about humans than malicious. That being said, if a shark is spotted nearby, it is better to be safe than sorry and get out of the water.

Let's draw a...

HARBOR SEAL

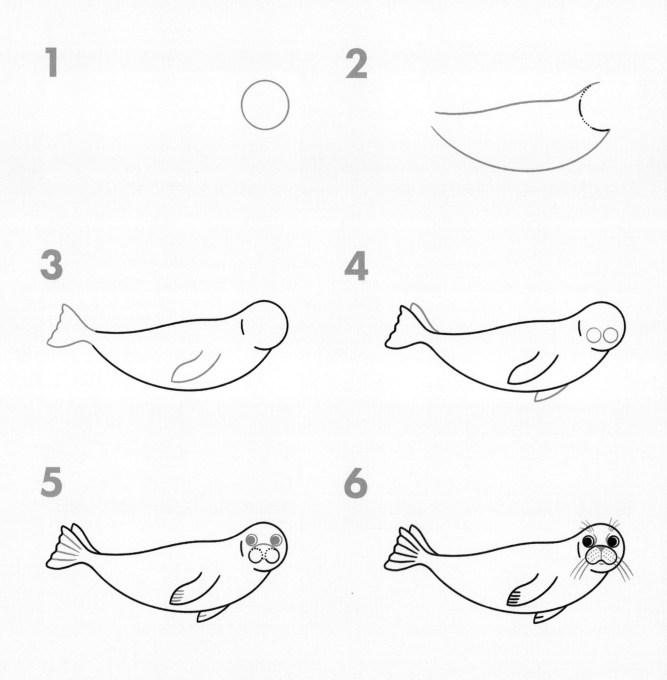

1

2

3

4

5

6

Harbors seals are large marine mammals with up to six-foot-long oval bodies. Their limbs are hidden within their body with only their webbed hands and feet, or flippers, extending. Harbor seals have round heads with no protruding ears and a short snout with V-shaped nostrils.

OBSERVATIONS

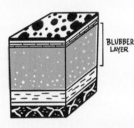

BLUBBER LAYER

Harbor seals spend half of their lives on land and half in the water. Their bodies are adapted to diving into deep waters — up to 1,500 feet deep! They have external pinnae, or openings to the ear canal, that close when they dive to keep water out. They also have a layer of blubber covering their bodies to keep them warm in the cold, deep water.

Unlike humans, harbor seals breathe out to dive and can hold their breath for up to half an hour! Breathing out helps them to be able to dive deeper. While underwater they rely on the oxygen stored in their blood until they resurface.

- 30 min -

Harbor seals have large, dark, round eyes that allow them to see well underwater. Their eyes are almost flat and dilate to let in as much light as possible in the dark. They also have a layer of mucus to protect their eyes in the water. When on land, they have terrible eyesight.

Harbor seals have long whiskers that detect underwater vibrations, helping them find food. Their whiskers are wavy to better cut through the water. They can detect the size of the vibration not only alerting the harbor seal to nearby food, but also telling it the size and direction of their prey.

TIP:

Harbor seals can be spotted during early morning low tides sitting on large rocks or the beach.

Let's draw a...

SEA OTTER

1

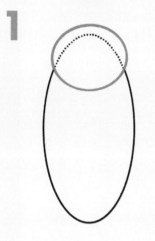

2

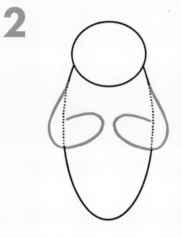

3

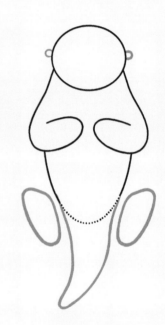

4

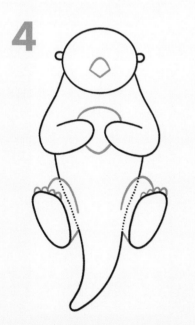

5

6

Sea otters are aquatic mammals in the weasel family. Their whole body is covered in fur that can range from brown to silver, except for their paw pads and nose. They can close their nostrils and ears in the water. Sea otters have long tails and big wide webbed back feet with small, webbed forepaws, making them excellent swimmers.

OBSERVATIONS

Sea otters have thicker fur than any other animal (800,000 to one million hairs per square inch). They don't have a layer of blubber like most aquatic mammals, so their fur helps keep them warm in the cold water. It is so dense that it traps air close to their body to create an insulated, waterproof layer. This bubble of air also makes them very buoyant, so they float effortlessly.

Sea otters use their long whiskers to hunt. Their whiskers are very sensitive and can sense vibrations in the water to help the otters find prey hidden in rock crevices. They eat shellfish like clams, mussels, crabs, and sea urchins, consuming 25 percent of their body weight every day.

Sea otters don't have flippers, but instead have webbed feet. These paws are useful for grabbing, digging, twisting, pulling, and even holding tools that they use to open their shelled food. They store these tools (usually a rock) in a pouch under their armpit.

Sea otters spend almost all their lives in the water, rarely leaving the ocean. They eat, sleep, and even have babies in the ocean. They rest in groups called rafts, split up into genders and held together by seaweed or by holding hands.

Let's draw a...

SEASHELL

1

2

3

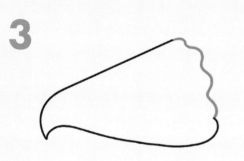

4

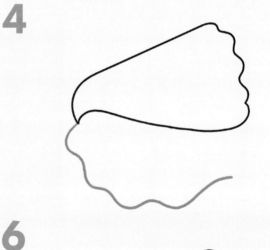

5

6

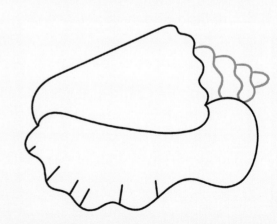

Seashells are the hard exoskeleton of mollusks such as snails, oysters, and clams. There are over 100,000 different mollusks species that create and live inside shells. Each kind of shell is unique — they can be round, tubular, smooth, bumpy, short, long, and spiraled.

OBSERVATIONS

Seashells are made from calcium carbonate. A mollusk produces the calcium carbonate and creates the shell layer by layer. The shape of the seashell depends on where the mollusk lives and what kind of predators are in their environment. The specific shapes are to deter their specific predators.

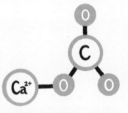

Shells can be univalve, made of one piece, or bivalved, made of two pieces. Univalve shells almost always open to the right and coil to the right. Shells can be tiny or huge like the Australian Trumpet Shell that averages around 35 inches.

Seashells come in many different colors and patterns. The colors come from what the mollusk eats and what is in their environment. The different colors and patterns work to camouflage the mollusk and their shell on the ocean floor and in coral.

FACT:
Mollusks that have shells build their shell their entire life.

Let's draw a...
CLAM

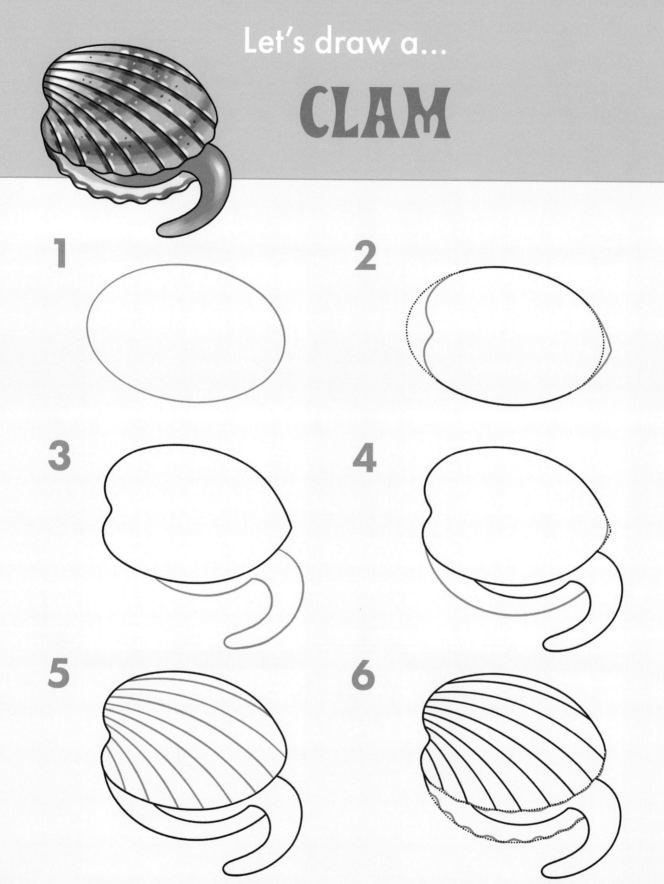

1

2

3

4

5

6

Clams are mollusks that build and live in bivalved shells, which means they are made of two pieces. Clam shells are typically triangular and connected at a joint with a rounded long edge and rings around the outside.

OBSERVATIONS

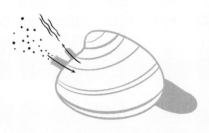

Clams siphon water into their shells to feed on the plankton, algae, and bacteria in the water around them. This process is called filter feeding and the particles that the clam eat are trapped by small hairs in their gills called cilia that move the particles to their mouths to eat. This process also helps clean the water in their environment

Clams have a single foot that they use to dig and move. They open their shell enough to stick the foot out and scoot sideways with it. The foot also digs by moving rapidly to burrow under the sand and hold them in place.

Clams come in many different sizes and there are thousands of different types. The largest clam in the world is the giant clam that can grow to be four feet wide and 500 pounds. Another clam, called a geoduck, has a six-to-eight-inch shell, but an extra-long neck called a siphon that can reach three feet and can't fit in the shell.

FACT:
Clams have no head, eyes, or brain and none of the five senses.

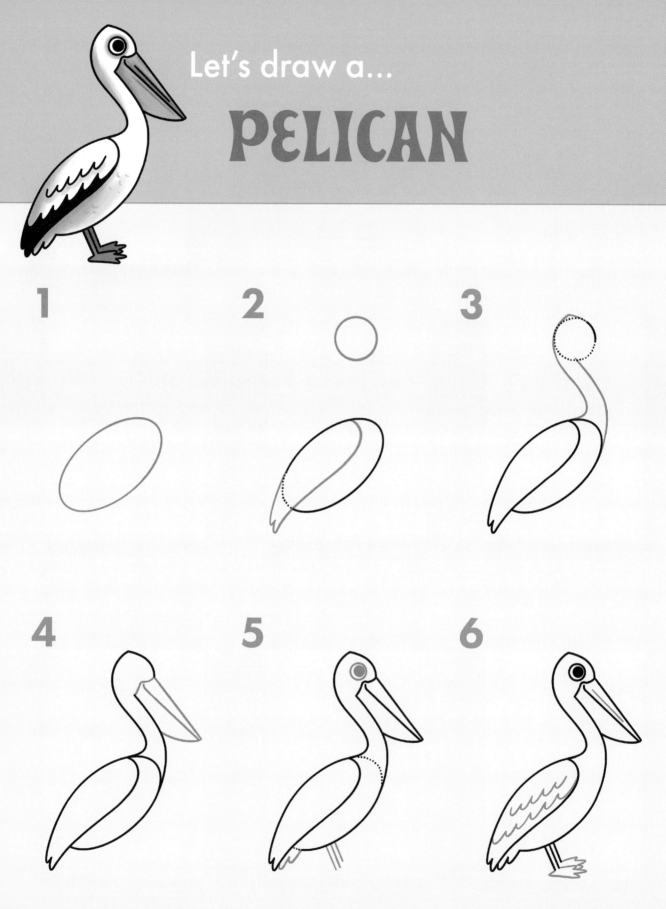

Let's draw a...

PELICAN

1

2

3

4

5

6

Pelicans are large birds found along the coast and coastal lakes and rivers. Most are white but can have yellow, black, brown, and gray feathers. Pelicans are known for their long necks and bill and extendable throat pouch used for scooping fish out of the water. They have extra-long wingspans and short webbed feet.

OBSERVATIONS

Pelicans hunt by using their throat pouch as a nest to scoop up fish. They then use muscles in their pouch to drain the water out and swallow their prey whole. They mostly eat fish but will also eat crayfish, amphibians, and sometimes small mammals.

Pelicans can have a wingspan of more than 10 feet depending on the species. They are the heaviest flying birds, but their long wings make them excellent fliers and allow them to carry their large bodies plus a mouth full of fish and water when hunting.

Pelicans have four fully webbed toes that they use as paddles when swimming. This is unique because most aquatic birds have three webbed toes and one backward facing toe. Pelicans also use their feet to takeoff out of the water by pounding their feet on the surface in unison while flapping their wings to generate speed for takeoff. Due to their size, pelicans need a little extra help to stay afloat. Their skeleton has air pockets to make them buoyant like a built-in lifejacket. They also have air pockets under the skin beneath their wings.

FACT:
While they look like pterodactyls, pelicans are descended from dinosaurs and have been on Earth for 30 million years!

Let's draw a...

SANDPIPER

1

2

3

4

5

6

Sandpipers are small to medium birds usually seen on beaches near the water. They have rounded long bodies with short tails and long narrow wings. They are gray or brown and sometimes spotted on top and white underneath. Sandpipers have long legs perfect for wading in the water and long, thin bills.

OBSERVATIONS

Sandpipers use their long bills to poke into sand and mud and find food. Their bills are flexible and can feel for food as they probe the beach. They then grab and pull their prey out of the sand. They eat insects, small crustaceans, snails, and worms that hide in the sand and mud.

Most kinds of sandpipers live and migrate in flocks that fly in synchronized patterns turning and landing in unison. They migrate long distances between North and South America. They are talented navigators and use magnetic fields to know where to go.

Sandpipers are known for a behavior called teetering. Teetering is when they bob their tail up and down rhythmically, like a dance. Scientists are unsure why they do this, but even baby sandpipers teeter.

Sandpipers usually build nests on the ground hiding in vegetation close to the shore. The female lays three to five spotted eggs in the spring. Baby sandpipers learn to feed themselves by following their parents.

FACT:
Sandpipers are very important to the ecosystems along the coast. They control the populations of the creatures they hunt.

Let's draw an...
OCTOPUS

1

2

3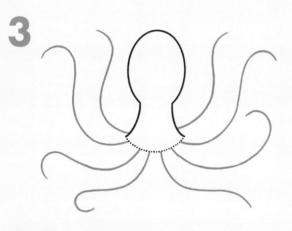

4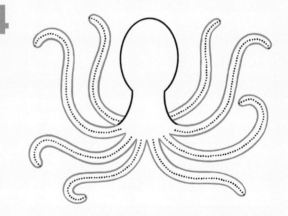

5

6

Octopus are cephalopods with eight arms covered in two rows of suckers. They have bulbous (round) heads and large bulging eyes. Octopus change color but are normally yellow, red, or brown. Octopus can range in size from the tiny one-inch long Wolfi octopus to the Giant Pacific octopus that can be up to 30 feet across.

OBSERVATIONS

Octopus can change their color faster than any other animal on the planet. In the blink of an eye, they can change colors and patterns to blend into their environment. This ability comes in handy when they need to hide from predators, since octopus do not have shells or hard bodies.

Octopus use their arms to quickly pounce on and grab their prey. They have a retractable beak on their underside in the center of their arms that they use to inject venom and break open shells and tear their food.

When in danger, octopus can squirt out black ink. This ink confuses their predators, burns their eyes, and temporarily makes the predator unable to taste and smell. The ink allows the octopus time to escape.

Octopus suckers are grooved to create an airtight grip on whatever they attach to. These suckers are used for more than just grabbing prey. Their suckers also have taste and touch sensors on them to help octopus explore the ocean around them.

FACT:
Octopus are great problem solvers and have been known to solve puzzles and mazes and tricky escapes.

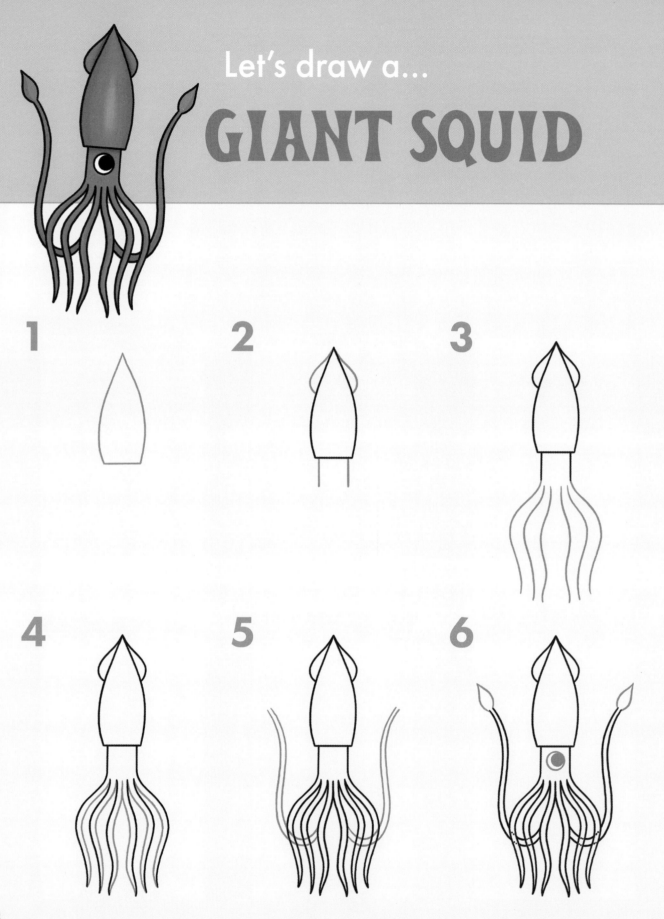

Let's draw a...

GIANT SQUID

1

2

3

4

5

6

Giant squids have been featured in stories from authors and sailors throughout history (the Kraken may be based on a giant squid), but it wasn't until 2006 that anyone even caught a video of one alive. These massive squid are the largest cephalopods on Earth and can grow larger than 42 feet (13 meters) to the end of their tentacles with their body (mantle) taking about seven feet of that length.

OBSERVATIONS

Giant squid look a lot like other squid, just...bigger. They have eight arms and two tentacles that are longer than their arms. These tentacles are used for catching their prey and bringing it to their beak-like mouth. The arms and tentacles of the squid are covered in suckers to trap their prey. Their suckers are lined with a serrated ring of chitin (the same thing our fingernails are made of) that digs into their prey. They also use these suckers to protect themselves from their only predator: the sperm whale.

Giant squid have the largest eye in the animal kingdom. Their eyes are as big as a basketball – about 10 inches in diameter. They need such large eyes to be able to see in the dark depths of the ocean that they live in. Having a large eye lets in more light allowing them to see shadows of moving creatures hundreds of feet from them in the ocean.

Giant squid move through the water using jet propulsion. They suck water into a tube in their mantle, called a siphon, and push it back out to shoot them forward. They use the small fins on the top of their head to steer. This allows them to maneuver around the deep waters (between 1,000 and 7,500 feet deep).

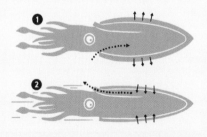

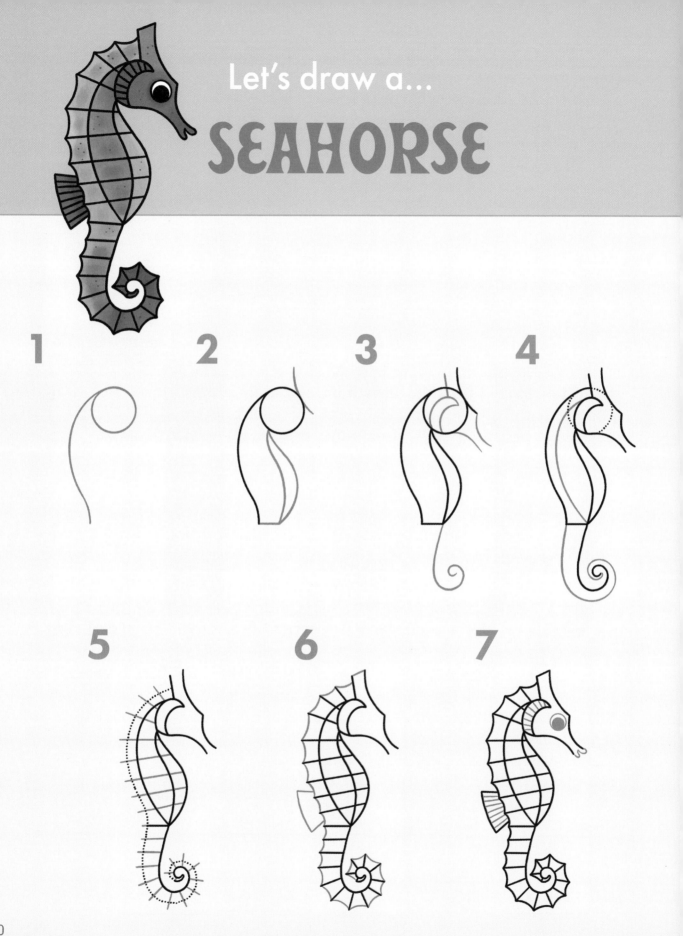

Let's draw a...

SEAHORSE

1

2

3

4

5

6

7

Seahorses are small fish with horse-like heads, hence the name. They have round bodies and a long, curved tail. Seahorses have four fins, one on either side of their face, one on their belly, and a fin at the base of their tail. Their whole body is covered in spiny plates from tail to head.

OBSERVATIONS

Seahorses are the slowest swimmers of all fish. Their back fin is too small to propel them anywhere and moves so rapidly that it can exhaust a seahorse quickly. Despite lack of speed, camouflaging ability and hydrodynamic head shape help them catch their prey.

To make up for being poor swimmers seahorses use their tail as a valuable tool. They can attach their flexible tail to floating plants to hitchhike rides around the ocean or anchor themselves to stationary plants to stay in place.

Seahorses spend most of their day eating and are known to eat about 30 "meals" a day, which equals about 3,000 brine shrimp daily. They don't have teeth or a stomach, so they pass food through their bodies very quickly. Their mouths work like a trap door that opens and then snaps closed quickly with a gulp to suck shrimp, plankton, and other small crustaceans into their bodies.

Seahorses mate for life, and the female seahorse gives the male seahorse the eggs to carry in his pouch until they are ready to hatch. Seahorses have around 2,000 babies, called a fry, at a time. These babies are born as teeny tiny fully formed seahorses.

CLOWNFISH

1

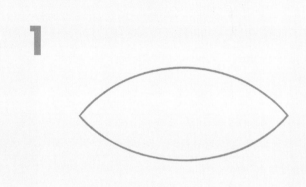

2

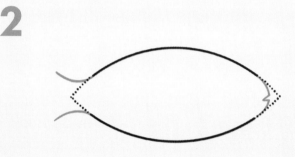

3

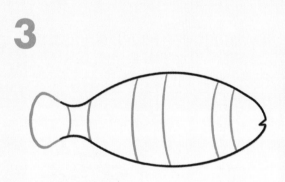

4

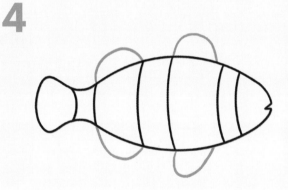

5

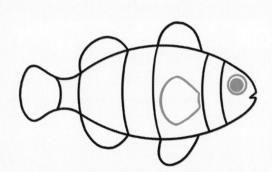

6

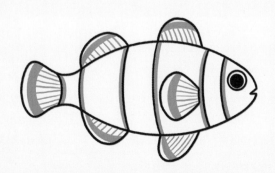

Clownfish are one of the most recognizable fish for their distinct coloring. They are bright orange with three white stripes in the center, at the tail, and on the head. The orange and white are separated by thick black bands that outline the orange portions.

OBSERVATIONS

Clownfish have a symbiotic relationship with anemone. A mucus on their body protects them from getting stung so they can hide from predators in the anemone's tentacles. The clownfish cleans the anemone, provides nutrients from their waste, and chases away fish that try to eat the anemone like butterflyfish.

Clownfish are very social and even speak their own language. They communicate with each other through popping and clicking sounds. These sounds are made by chattering their jaws or shaking their heads.

Most clownfish are male. They live in groups with one female and many males. The female lays hundreds of eggs and then the males protect the eggs. They fan the eggs with their fins to increase oxygen around them and clean them with their mouth to stop algae growth.

Clownfish are not strong swimmers. They spend a lot of time hiding in the anemone from predators and don't tend to venture far. They swim by rowing their pectoral fins and can be erratic in their movements.

FACT:
All clownfish are born males. If there are no females in their group, a clownfish can change into a female.

Let's draw a...
PUFFER FISH

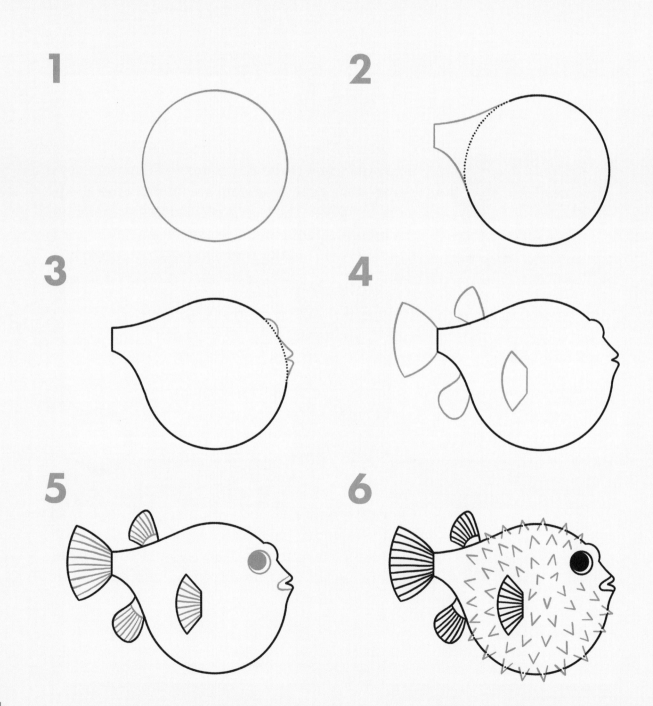

1

2

3

4

5

6

Puffer fish are known by many names including balloonfish, blowfish, and swellfish. When not puffed up, they are typically oval, streamlined scaleless fish covered in spines or prickly skin. They can be spotted or striped. When in danger, they can puff their bodies into a balloon-like ball three times their size.

OBSERVATIONS

Puffer fish are known for their ability to inflate with water or air. When they sense danger, the pufferfish will gulp air or water into their elastic stomachs. This makes it difficult for predators to bite them. If their spikes and inflation don't work to deter predators, puffer fish are usually also toxic. Their poison tastes bad and can even kill predators who try to eat them. They are so poisonous, that touching a puffer fish can kill humans.

Puffer fish's teeth are fused together into a beak that constantly grows. They use their teeth to scrape algae off rocks, which also helps to keep their teeth ground down. They also use their hard beak-like teeth to crack open and eat clams, shellfish, crabs, and muscles.

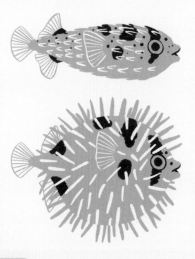

Male pufferfish make giant decorative nests to attract mates. They use their bellies and fins to create geometric patterns in a large circle. They also often decorate their nest with shells. They never use the same nest twice.

FACT:
Pufferfish don't have eyelids but can close their eyes by sucking them into their sockets.

Let's draw a...

LOBSTER

1

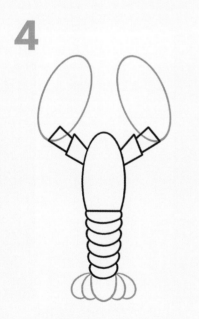

2

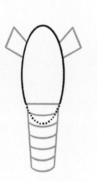

3

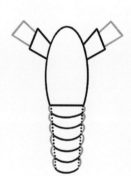

4

5

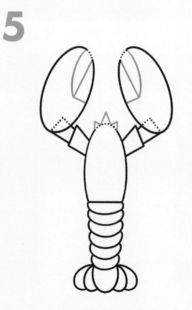

6

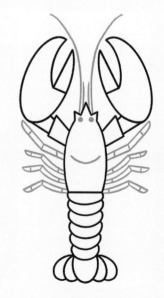

Lobsters are large shrimp-like crustaceans with five pairs of legs, the front set taking the form of large claws. Their bodies are long and broken into segments covered in a hard shell and ending in wide flat tail fins. Lobsters have three pairs of antennae and eyes on stalks.

OBSERVATIONS

Lobsters can be many different colors and usually range from brown to green, blue, or orange. People usually think they are red due to the red color they turn when exposed to heat. Their blood is even blue due to the molecules in their blood.

Lobsters do not have vocal cords but are still able to communicate with each other in an interesting way: their urine. Lobsters urinate at each other from an opening near their antennae. Chemicals in their urine tell other lobsters' messages such as who is in charge, when it's time to mate, and when they are stressed.

Lobsters' eyes likely only detect light, so they depend on their antennas to "see" the ocean around them. The four small antennas detect chemicals and movement in the water. The large pair of antennas feel around them.

Lobster's claws are different sizes. The smaller claw is for pinching and ripping apart prey, the large claw is for crushing prey. They also use their claws for fighting off predators and other lobsters.

FACT:
Lobsters grow through molting (just like crabs) and can live for over 100 years!

LIONFISH

1

2

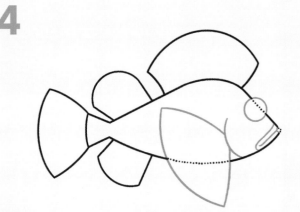

3

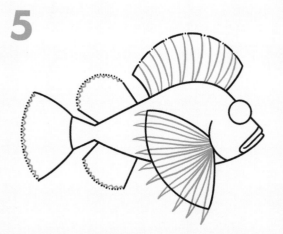

4

5

6

58

Lionfish are striped fish found in coral reefs. They are brown to maroon with white stripes covering their whole body, fins, and spines. They have 18 spines, up to 18 rays, and tentacles above their head and under their mouth. They are called lionfish due to the lion's mane appearance of all the spines and rays.

OBSERVATIONS

Lionfish are nocturnal (night) predators that hunt all kinds of fish, mollusks, and crustaceans. They have big appetites, and their stomach can expand up to 30 times its regular size. They sometimes go weeks without eating, but when they do hunt, they can eat one to two fish a minute.

The spines covering lionfish are venomous. Due to these spines, lionfish have almost no predators, especially in the Atlantic Ocean where they are not native. Sharks are one of their few predators and are immune to the lionfish's venom.

Lionfish grow to be about 15 inches, but make themselves look much larger with their tentacles, spines, and rays fanned out. Due to their bright coloration, they don't have the ability to blend into their surroundings, so they rely on a larger physical appearance for protection.

Lionfish are slow and don't chase their prey. They instead persistently follow their prey until they can stretch out their fins and corner them. They are territorial and males will fight other male lionfish who enter their territory.

FACT:
Lionfish are expanding into non-native habitats and killing off entire populations of fish in reefs. This is why people should never dump aquariums.

Let's draw a...

MORAY EEL

1

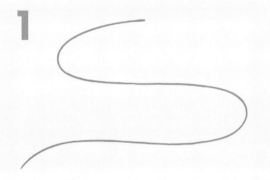

2

3

4

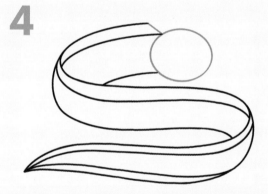

5

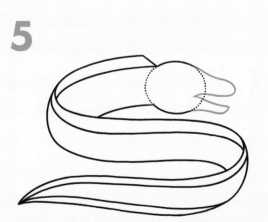

6

The moray eel is a long snake-like fish with a dorsal fin that starts behind its head and extends along its whole body. Moray eels are usually around five feet long, but some can grow over ten feet long. They have small eyes, two nostril holes, and a long toothy mouth.

OBSERVATIONS

Moray eels look green due to a layer of yellow mucus that covers their body, but they are actually brownish gray or blue. The mucus makes them slimy and able to slip their bodies into crevices and between coral to hide. It also protects them from parasites and bacteria.

Moray eels have two sets of jaws. The first jaw has a set of sharp teeth to catch the prey and keep them from escaping. The second jaw then juts out to then pull the prey into their throat. Moray eels have an incredibly strong bite capable of a lot of force.

Moray eels have bad eyesight but they make up for it with a great sense of smell. They can smell injured or dead animals in the reef to track down and eat. They are essential to keeping the reef clean.

Moray eels constantly open and close their mouths. This is their way of breathing. Instead of breathing through gills like most fish, moray eels must pump water over the gill chamber in their body to breathe.

FACT:
Moray eels do not usually attack people but have been known to bite fingers off divers due to their poor eyesight.

Let's draw a...
PARROTFISH

1

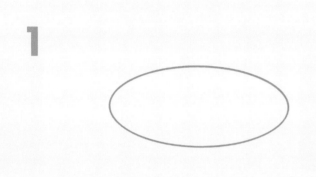

2

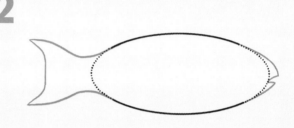

3

4

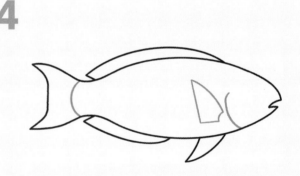

5

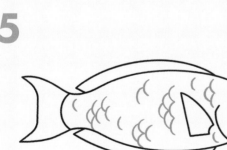

6

Parrotfish, a group of fish named for their beak-like fused teeth and bright colors, are found in reefs worldwide. Parrotfish come in many different bright colors and patterns. They are usually around 20 inches long but some species can grow over four feet long. Most parrotfish have blunt faces.

OBSERVATIONS

Parrotfish are covered in large colorful scales that are sometimes very thick. Their colors change throughout their life as they age, become more dominant in their groups, or change gender. Most parrotfish start female but can change gender (and color) if needed.

Parrotfish use their beak-like teeth to eat algae. To do this they have to break off chunks of coral and grind them in their strong teeth. They then excrete the ground up coral as a fine sand. Parrotfish can excrete hundreds of pounds of sand each year.

Parrotfish protect themselves while sleeping by making a "sleeping bag" of mucus. Special glands in their gills secrete a clear mucus that they encapsulate themselves in to keep parasitic animals from attaching to them at night. It also hides their smell from predators.

FACT:
When you enjoy white sand beaches, remember that over 70 percent of the sand came from parrotfish.

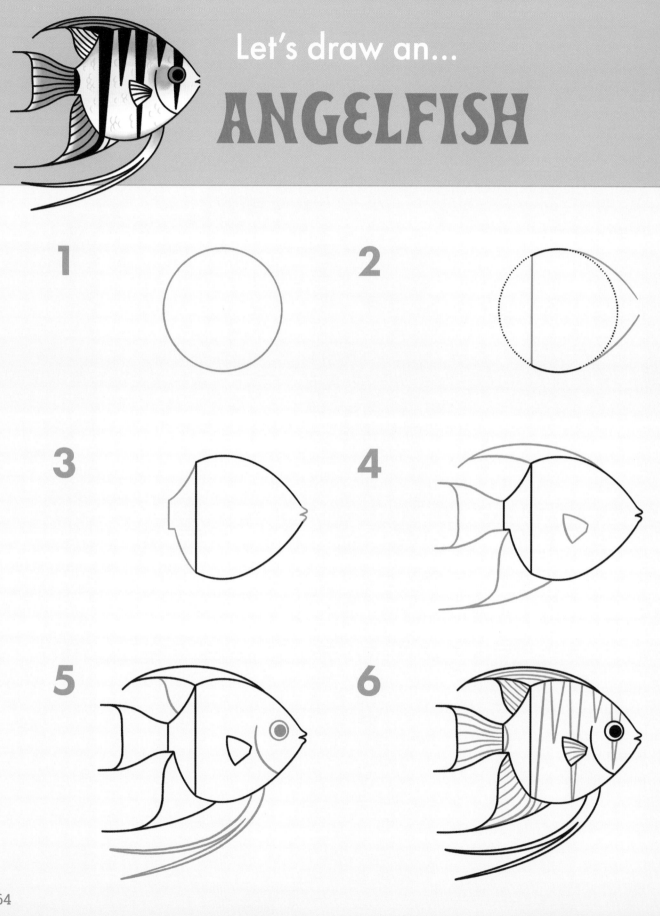

Let's draw an...

ANGELFISH

1

2

3

4

5

6

Marine angelfish are colorful fish with long dorsal and anal fins. They are named for the shape their body makes when viewed sideways: the head, dress, and wings of an angel. They have small mouths and are usually around 12 inches long, though this can vary. They come in many different vivid colors.

OBSERVATIONS

Angelfish are found in tropical waters. There are 86 known species of angelfish all in varying colors, patterns, shapes, and sizes. Different markings can help angelfish camouflage or even appear bigger. Some angelfish have spots that look like large eyes to scare predators.

Angelfish are omnivores and opportunistic eaters, which means they will eat almost anything they can from algae to jellyfish. They have relatively small mouths, so they have to stick to smaller foods. Their favorite food is sponges, and they help control the spread of sea sponges by eating them.

Angelfish are solitary but are sometimes seen in pairs. When they lay eggs, the eggs float to the top of the water when the male angelfish fertilize them. The eggs then float in the currents until they hatch. Many eggs get eaten by other animals before they hatch.

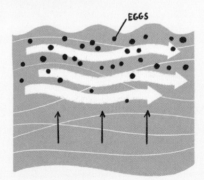

FACT:
Marine angelfish are known to be friendly and fearless and will often come right up to divers.

Let's draw a...

BUTTERFLYFISH

1

2

3

4

5

6

Butterflyfish are a colorful reef fish with rounded triangular bodies. They are thin from side to side and have tall bodies. Butterflyfish have long thin snouts that can vary in length between species.

OBSERVATIONS

There are more than 130 species of butterflyfish that vary in color and shape. Like some butterflies, some butterflyfish have a large spot on either side near their tail, or fake eye. This can confuse predators to think they are much larger or not know where their head is.

Butterflyfish are small and fast. They dart around in quick movements using their tail fin as a rudder to change direction quickly. These movements help them flit in and out of the coral to escape predators.

Butterflyfish are often found in pairs but can sometimes also live in very large groups. They eat coral polyps and require plentiful, healthy coral to live, so seeing many butterflyfish in a reef is a sign of a healthy reef.

Butterflyfish are carnivores and are opportunistic eaters. They eat crustaceans, sponges, coral polyps, worms, and even eat sea anemone. The stings of the sea anemone do not affect butterflyfish.

FACT:
Butterflyfish and angelfish used to be classified as the same family and share many attributes.

Let's draw a...

PUFFIN

1

2

3

4

5

6

Puffins are seabirds nicknamed "sea parrots" due to their bright orange and red parrot-like bill. They are short and stocky with a black body and short black tail and a white belly and chest. They also have a white face and cheeks. They are small, only about 12 inches long, and have orange webbed feet.

OBSERVATIONS

Puffins spend most of their life on the ocean. They can dive 200 feet underwater to catch fish using their feet to steer and their wings to fly through the water. They eat small fish, often catching many in one dive and holding them in their bill with the help of spines on the roof of their mouth and their rough tongue.

They are both great swimmers and great fliers. Puffins beat their wings rapidly when flying (up to 400 times a minute) and reach speeds of up to 55 miles per hour. When not in the air or diving, they float around in the waves of the ocean.

Puffins' bills change color in the spring to the bright color they are known for. The colorful bills are to show off during the breeding season. In the fall, they lose their colorful bill and it is replaced by a smaller, duller bill.

For the most part, puffins are very quiet. They stay silent at sea and even in their colonies. The males only get noisy during the breeding season. They make pig-like grunts and growls to attract females.

TIP:
The best time to spot a puffin is when they are on land for the spring mating season.

Let's draw a...
DAMSELFISH

1

2

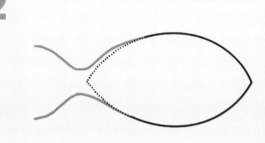

3

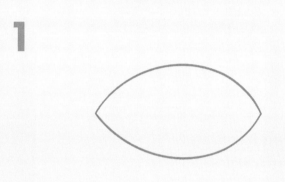

4

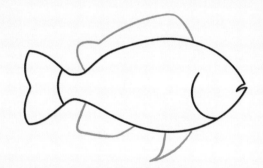

5

6

Damselfish are small reef deep-bodied fish, which means its body is tall from top to bottom. They usually have forked tails and spiny dorsal fins. Their scales are typically large and visible. Damselfish come in many color combinations but the most common are yellow, blue, orange, white, and black.

OBSERVATIONS

Damselfish are closely related to clownfish, and like clownfish many have a symbiotic relationship with anemone. The anemone gives the damselfish protection, and the damselfish eats the algae and gives the anemone food scraps.

Damselfish are aggressive and territorial. Though they are small, they will charge at other fish who are trying to invade their territory to scare them away. They will attack other damselfish in their territory other than their mate.

Most species of damselfish are monogamous, meaning they mate for life. They protect their homes and nests with their mate. Damselfish build nests by clearing rocks and sometimes using materials to shelter their eggs.

FACT:
Damselfish can be found in many different coastal habitats due to their ability to adapt.

Let's draw a...
FLOUNDER

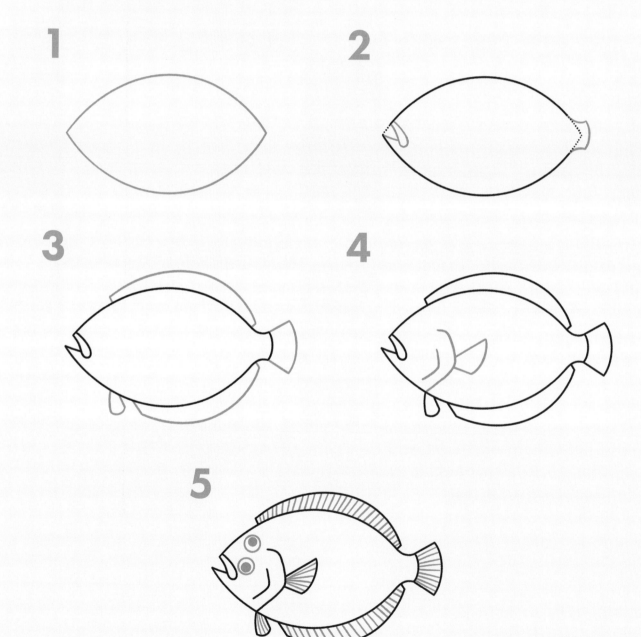

1

2

3

4

5

Flounders are medium sized, flat, disc-shaped fish. Both of their eyes are on the same side of their head and the color of their body varies depending on the side their eyes are on with the upper side darker and the bottom side lighter. Flounders are shades of brown with spots.

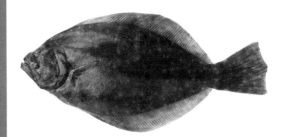

OBSERVATIONS

Flounders do not start out with their eyes on the same side. They lay flat on the ocean floor and as they grow, the eye facing down migrates to the other side. The side that faces up depends on the species of flounder.

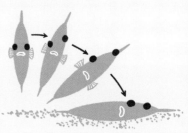

Flounder can change color to camouflage with their sur-roundings. They have cells similar to octopuses that al-low them to quickly change color. Their top side is always darker than their bottom side so when they swim up, they can blend in with the sunny surface from underneath.

Flounder are ambush predators and have small mouths filled with sharp, pointy teeth. They eat mostly small fish and are nocturnal, hunting at night. Flounders wait for a fish to swim over their camouflage body and then pounce.

Flounder swim sideways and use their fins to move around the ocean floor. They also use their fins to kick up sand and bury themselves in it to better hide from predators and their prey. When they bury themselves, they become so camouflage that their eyes are the only visible part of the body.

FACT:
Flounders with damaged or blind eyes cannot change colors to match their background, because they can't see it.

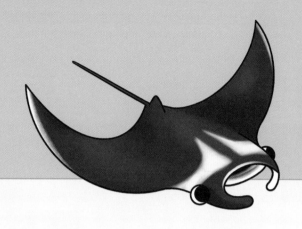

MANTA RAY

1

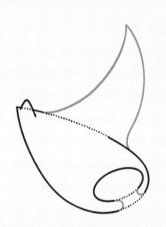

2

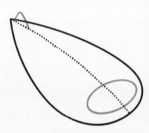

3

4

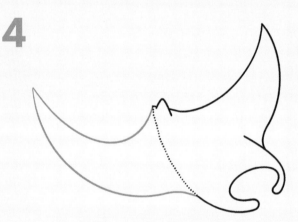

5

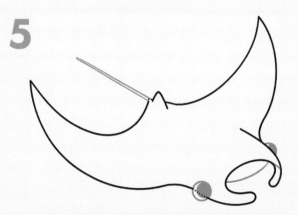

Manta rays are large diamond-shaped fish named for the Spanish word "manta," which means blanket or cloak. They are 15 to 30 feet in length and have pectoral fins that resemble wings with a long tail. Manta rays have large mouths with eyes on either side and two cephalic fins at the front of their bodies that look resemble dog ears.

OBSERVATIONS

The cephalic fins on the front of a manta ray's mouth are used for funneling food into their constantly open mouth while swimming. They eat tiny krill and zooplankton, filtering water out of their gill slits and the food into their mouths.

Manta rays are covered in a mucus layer. This layer keeps them protected from harmful bacteria. Without this mucus shield they are susceptible to illness, which is why even though they are harmless, you should never touch a manta ray.

If a manta ray stops swimming, they will die. Swimming forces water over their gills to extract oxygen and breathe. They also can never swim backward since only forward motion moves water over their gills.

Manta rays are very smart and social. They often swim and eat together and are known to have friendships with other rays. Manta rays jump out of the water "flying" through the air. Scientists don't understand why, but it may be a form of communication.

FACT:
Every manta ray has different markings on their underside that are as unique as fingerprints.

ANGLERFISH

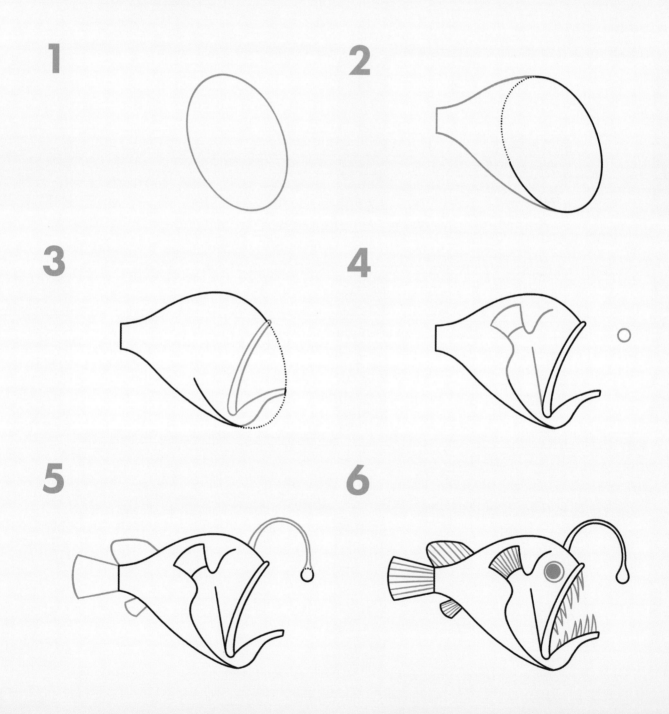

1

2

3

4

5

6

Anglerfish are medium to large greyish or brown fish that typically live in murky waters. They have large bulbous heads with very wide crescent-shaped mouths full of teeth. Anglerfish have a rod on the top of their head that ends in a lure.

OBSERVATIONS

Female anglerfish have a glowing lure that dangles from a rod in front of their head. The lure is filled with bioluminescent bacteria that the anglerfish can conceal or reveal with a skin flap. Unsuspecting prey such as fish and crustaceans are attracted to the lure and then pounced on by the anglerfish.

Male anglerfish are tiny and cannot survive without the female. After they develop, they attach themselves to their mate by their teeth, eventually fusing to the female's body and becoming a single symbiotic creature, dependent on the female for food.

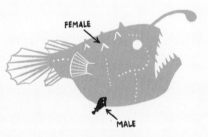

FEMALE

MALE

Anglerfish have two rows of sharp, translucent teeth. Their teeth point inward to trap their prey. They can catch and eat prey twice their size due to the ability to expand their stomach and jaw.

FACT:
Anglerfish can be found in both deep dark ocean and murky shallow waters.

Let's draw an...

ORCA

1

2

3

4

5

Orcas, also known as killer whales, are the largest species of dolphins. They are mostly black on top with a white belly and white patch above their small eyes, and usually a gray or white patch behind their dorsal fin called a saddle patch. Orcas have a blowhole similar to a nostril on top of their head for breathing and a mouth full of large sharp teeth (up to 4 inches long!).

OBSERVATIONS

Orcas are known for their black and white coloring. Their marks and coloring act as camouflage in the dark water. The unique shapes of their white spots and belly distort their outline so it is tricky to see their size or shape.

Their unique ability to blend in with the ocean makes orcas skilled hunters. They are known as apex predators, which means that they are on the top of the food chain. Orcas hunt in groups and coordinate their moves in the water working together to catch their prey.

Orcas speak their own language to communicate with each other. They "speak" through clicks, whistles, squeaks, squeals, and yells. Each orca family, or pod, has their own "language" that is different from other pods. Their clicks also come in handy for echolocation when hunting for their food under the water.

Orcas must come to the surface to breathe, so they need to stay awake all the time to remember to breathe. To do this, they can only allow half of their brain to sleep at a time. This also comes in handy to keep them always alert for dangers around them.

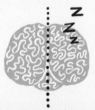

TIP:
Orcas can be found in every ocean. Other than humans, orcas are the most widely distributed mammal in the world — which means you can find them everywhere!

Let's draw a...

SEA TURTLE

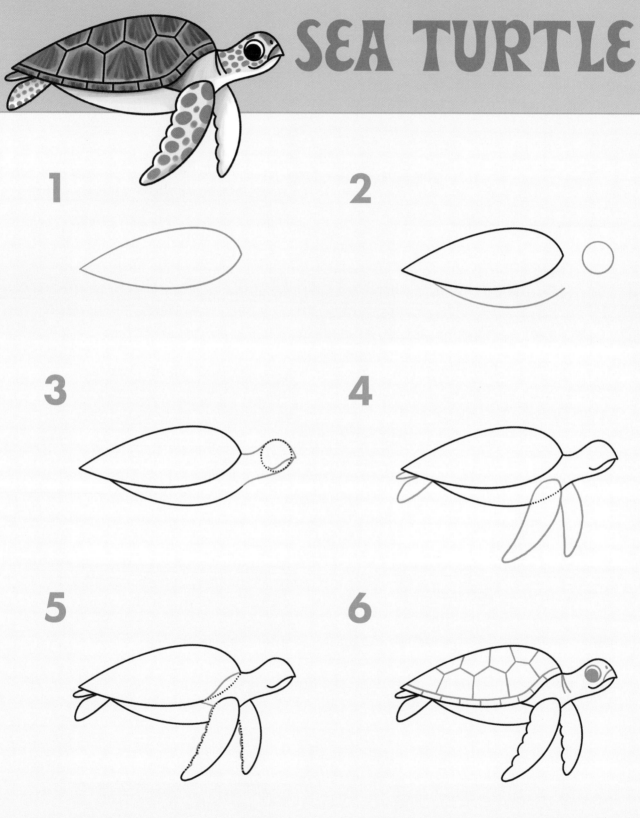

1

2

3

4

5

6

Sea turtles have large teardrop shaped shells and two pairs of flippers and a tail. Their heads are sleek and oval with a sharp beak mouth. Sea turtles have large eyes and eye-lids. Sea turtle limbs do not retract into their bodies like other turtles.

OBSERVATIONS

Sea turtles grow from a tiny two-inch baby hatchlings to three to six feet long depending on the species. Their journey to life is difficult and only 1 in 1,000 live to be adults, but if they do make it, sea turtles live long lives, from 50 to 100 years old!

Sea turtles memorize the location of their nests when they are born using the Earth's magnetic fields. When they are adults (around 30 years) they migrate thousands of miles across the oceans to return to the locations of their nests to mate and lay eggs.

Sea turtle do not have teeth. They use their hard beak shaped mouth to grab and eat food. What they eat depends on the species and can range from a herbivore, carnivore, or omnivore diet.

Sea turtle shells are bony and very strong and protect them from predators. Their bones are light-weight and spongy though to keep them buoyant and help them float. Every sea turtle's shell is completely unique and identifiable from another.

FACT:
Most of a sea turtle's life is spent in the ocean in coastal waters and drifting in open sea.

MAHI MAHI

1

2

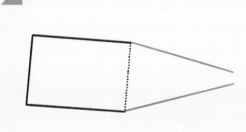

3

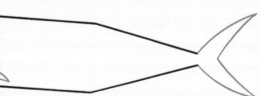

4

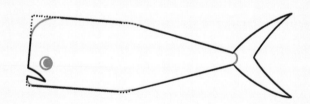

5

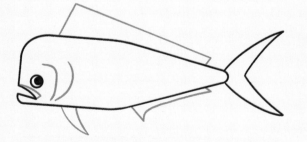

6

Mahi mahi, also known as the dolphinfish, is a long fish with a big blunt head. Female mahi mahi heads are smaller and rounder and males have protruding foreheads. Mahi mahi are metallic green with yellow and blue details with a mohawk-like dorsal fin that runs their whole body and a tall forked caudal (back) fin.

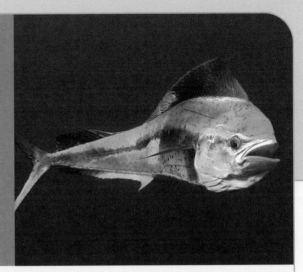

OBSERVATIONS

Mahi mahi means "strong" in Hawaiian and is named to describe their strong swimming. Mahi mahi can swim up to 40 miles per hour due to their forked tail. They use their strong swimming to migrate across the ocean traveling north in the summer and south in the winter.

Mahi mahi grow extremely quickly. They grow to full adult size in a single year, growing about two and a half inches a week. They are typically around 40 inches long but have been found much larger (up to seven feet long).

Mahi mahi eat all kinds of fish, crustaceans, and squid but their favorite meal is the flying fish. The mahi mahi chase the flying fish on the surface of the water, gobbling them up as they dive back under. Flying fish make up about a quarter of the mahi mahi's diet.

FACT:
Mahi mahi like warm waters and are typically found near the surface.

Let's draw a...
HERMIT CRAB

1

2

3

4

5

6

Hermit crabs are decapod crustaceans, meaning they have five pairs of legs, including their front claws. Hermit crabs only have their claws and two pair of legs visible, with their other two pairs of legs holding their found shells in place. They have two eyes on stalks and two pairs of antennae.

OBSERVATIONS

Hermit crabs do not have their own shells and use empty snail shells or other objects as their shelter. They do not have a hard body and rely on these found shells to protect them. When they grow out of their shell, they simply find a new, bigger one.

Hermit crab claws are different sizes. The big claw is used for fighting off predators and blocking their shell entrance. The smaller claw is used for catching and shredding food, which is basically anything they can find.

Hermit crabs live in large groups of 100 or more. They keep each other safer from predators by living in these groups. They also socialize with other animals such as sea anemone and ragworm, which sometimes live on and in their shells with them.

Hermit crabs have eye stalks that can move and see independently of each other. They can see all around them to watch for predators and food. They also use their antennae to get a sense of their surroundings with the longer pair feeling and the shorter pair tasting and smelling.

FACT:
Hermit crabs will trade shells and hand down shells that are too small to other hermit crabs.

Let's draw a...

HAMMERHEAD SHARK

1

2

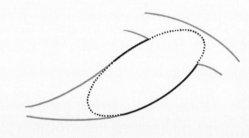

3

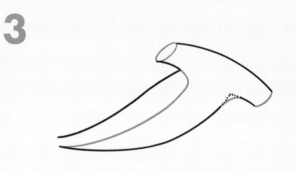

4

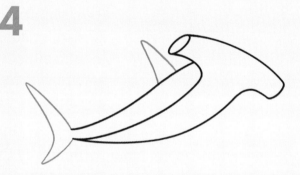

5

6

Hammerhead sharks are sharks with very unusually shaped heads. The front of their head is shaped like a long thin rectangle with their eyeballs on either end and a large crescent mouth underneath. Their heads can go straight across either angled like an arrow or rounded. They are grayish brown to green on top with a white underside.

OBSERVATIONS

Hammerhead shark's head shape helps it better scan the ocean for its favorite prey: stingrays. Their head has sensors along it that can sense electrical signals of the shark's prey. Having their eyes on the ends of their wide head helps them see more of the ocean floor at once.

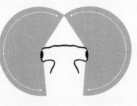

When a hammerhead shark finds a stingray, they chase and pin it to the ocean floor with their heads to eat it. Hammerheads sharks have 17 rows of triangular serrated teeth (like a saw). They also eat fish, crustaceans, squid, and even other sharks.

Hammerhead sharks almost have 360-degree vision with the only exception being a blind spot in front of their nose. They can see to the sides, above, below, and behind them all at once. Their pupils also dilate in low light, helping them to see even in the dark. Hammerhead sharks can swim sideways and do so most of the time. Sideways swimming conserves energy and reduces fin drag to make them more efficient swimmers. Their pectoral fins and dorsal fins are all similar lengths allowing them to roll to their sides.

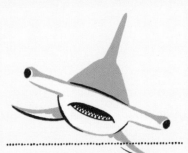

FACT:
Hammerhead sharks have never killed a human — their great vision helps them not confuse people with prey.

Let's draw a...

STINGRAY

1

2

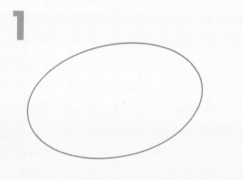

3

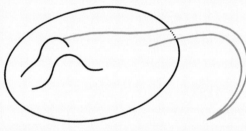

4

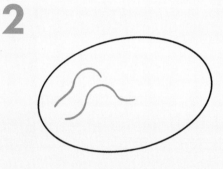

5

Stingrays are flat, disc shaped fish whose head come to a point and side fins extend out like wings. Stingray's eyes are on the top of its body, and their mouths are underneath. Stingray tails are long and contain a serrated venomous barb.

OBSERVATIONS

Stingray coloring depends on the species. Most are brownish yellow to blend into the sand. Some have spots, and one kind of stingray even has bright blue spots. The patterns on their backs help them to blend into the ocean floor.

Stingrays have eyes on the top of their head to spot predators when they are hiding in the sand. If a predator finds them, they use their venomous barb to defend themselves. They only use their barb for self-defense, and not as a hunting tool.

Stingrays mostly eat small animals that live in the sand. They suck their prey up like snails, worms, crustaceans, and shellfish into their mouth by creating a vacuum with their gills and jaw. They have strong jaws to crunch and chew their often hard food.

Stingrays have no bones and are made completely of cartilage. To swim they wave their bendy bodies or flap their fins like wings to move around. They can also jump out of the water and fly through the air!

FACT:
A group of stingrays is called a fever.

Let's draw a...

SHRIMP

1

2

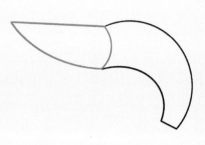

3

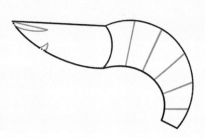

4

5

6

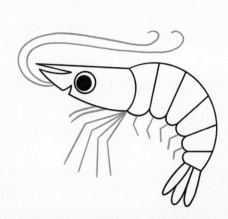

Shrimp are small crustaceans closely related to the lobster. They have long thin bodies that are segmented from the abdomen to the tail. Shrimp have five pairs of legs and five pairs of swimmerets. They have two pairs of antennae, one long and one short, and three pairs of maxillae (feeding arms).

OBSERVATIONS

Despite not having any fins, shrimp are great swimmers. They have swimmerets, which are special paddle-like legs and flex their tail and abdomen to move them through the water. They can swim forward, but mostly swim backwards because it is more natural for their bodies and faster.

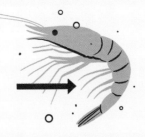

 Shrimp are found in every ocean and sea in the world and at every depth from shallow to deep water. There are about 2,000 species of shrimp of all sizes, colors, and characteristics. They can live in freezing water and lava-heated water.

Shrimp eat anything they can find on the bottom of the ocean. They don't hunt and instead scavenge for algae, plants, and dead or living animals that they come across on the ocean floor. The color of a shrimp can change depending on what they eat and the environment they are in.

Shrimp have hard shells, or exoskeletons, like other crustaceans. As they grow, they shed their old shell and grow a new one in a process called molting. Their molted shell is usually transparent.

FACT:
Shrimp are an important part of the ocean ecosystem. They are a food source for many animals and sometimes also remove bacteria and parasites from other animals.

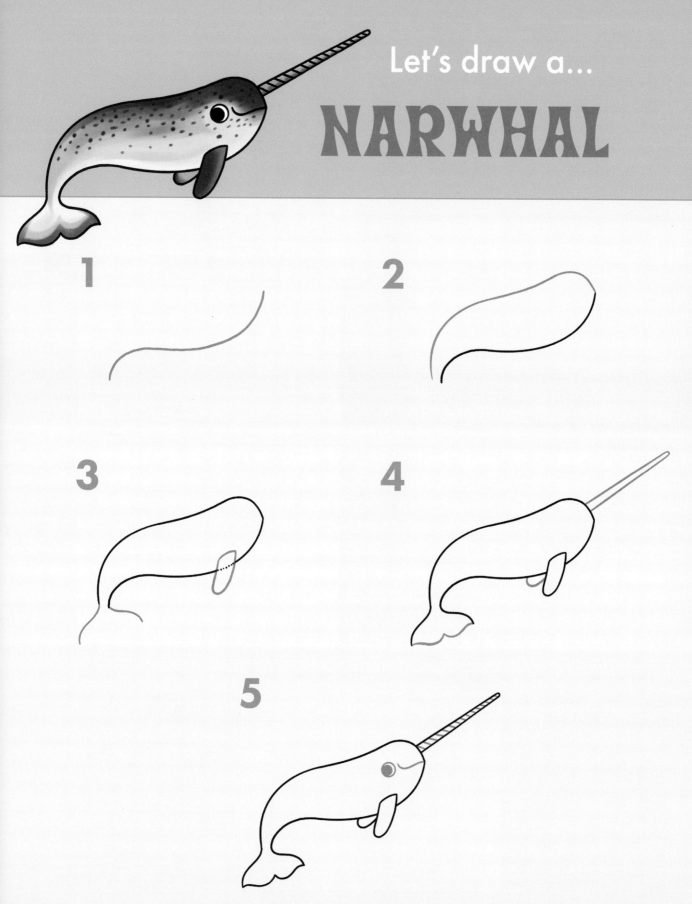

Let's draw a...

NARWHAL

1

2

3

4

5

Narwhals are arctic whales known as the "unicorns of the sea" because of their long, straight, spiraled tusk. They have long torpedo-like bodies. Narwhals have small eyes, small fins, and fan-shaped tail called a fluke.

OBSERVATIONS

The narwhal's tusk, which looks like a horn coming out of its head, is actually a tooth – the narwhal's only tooth. It is very sensitive and can sense when prey is nearby, and changes in the water such as temperature and salt level.

A narwhal's tusk continues to grow throughout their life and can grow up to 10 feet long. Most males have a tusk and sometimes females do as well. Some narwhals have two tusks, but this is rare. Their tusk grows in a counterclockwise spiral.

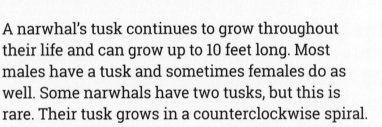

10FT

Narwhals change color as they age. Babies are blue gray, getting darker as they get older. Adults are mottled, or spotted, dark gray. Old narwhals are white. Narwhals' color helps them hide from predators like orcas and polar bears.

Narwhals live in the arctic under the ice. They are mammals and breathe air, so they come out of the water at cracks in the ice to breathe. They can dive very deep in the water and hold their breath for up to 25 minutes.

FACT:
Scientists still have a lot to learn about narwhals and are discovering more about them each year.

Let's draw a...
WALRUS

1

2

3

4

5

6

Walruses are large, brown to red, wrinkly blubbery arctic mammals. They have two front oar-shaped flippers and a long back flipper. Walruses have two large tusks protruding down from their mouth. They have long whiskers and very small eyes and ears.

OBSERVATIONS

Walrus are covered in a thick layer of blubber. The only part of their body not covered in blubber are their flippers. Their blubber keeps them warm in the freezing arctic temperatures that they live in. Their blubber is covered with wrinkly skin that is thick enough to protect them from the ice.

Both male and female walruses have tusks. Their tusks are extra-long teeth. Walruses use their tusks to protect themselves, fight, dig through the sediment on the ocean floor, and climb onto ice.

Walruses have hundreds of whiskers on their face, called vibrissae. These whiskers are short, thick, and very sensitive. Walruses have poor eyesight, so they rely on their whisker to detect food like clams and other shellfish on the ocean floor.

Walruses prefer to rest on the beach or ice but can actually sleep in the ocean if there is nowhere to rest nearby. They have pouches on their throats called pharyngeal pouches that fill with air like a lifejacket and keep them floating while sleeping.

FACT:
Walruses are social and live in giant herds of 100 or more.

Let's draw a...

TUNA

1

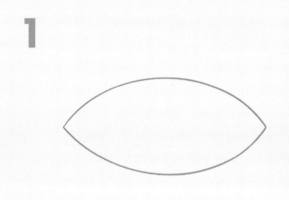

2

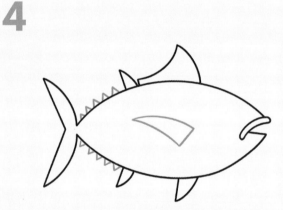

3

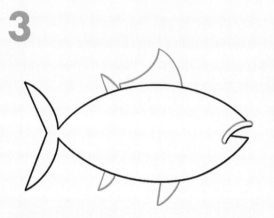

4

5

6

Tuna are very large fish, up to 13 feet long and 1,500 pounds! They are long and streamlined with a rounded head that tapers into a thin tail base. Tuna fish have many small fins called finlets following their dorsal fins. Tuna are iridescent and dark colored on top and white or silver on the bottom.

OBSERVATIONS

Tuna fish are some of the fastest fish in the ocean with speeds of over 45 miles per hour. Their speed is due to streamlined bodies and fins along with smooth scales. They migrate long distances and need to be able to travel quickly. Their speed also helps them escape predators and hunt.

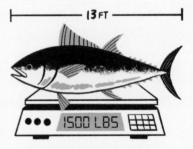

Tuna can never stop swimming. They require movement to pump water over their gills to breathe. They swim with their mouths open to pump the water through.

Tuna live and migrate in schools with hundreds or sometimes thousands of other tunas. Staying in schools protects the tuna from predators and helps them work together to hunt. Different species of tuna will sometimes be a part of the same school.

FACT:
Tuna are considered one of the top ocean predators and can outgrow sharks.

Let's draw a...

MARLIN

1

2

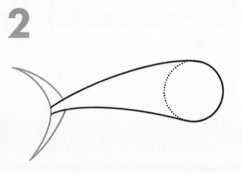

3

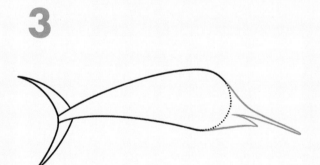

4

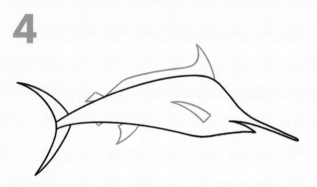

5

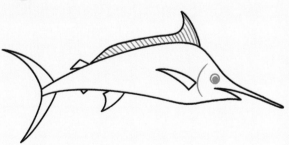

98

Marlins are long with an extra-long pointed bill. Their dorsal fin is rigid and starts out as a tall crest tapering down as it follows their entire bodies. They have tall, thin crescent shaped caudal (tail) fins. Marlins are dark blue on top, silver on the sides, and white underneath.

OBSERVATIONS

Marlins use their long, spear-like bill to catch fish by slashing them and stunning them unconscious. They can also spear fish with their bill and then shake them off to eat them. With their bill, marlins can reach lengths of over 12 feet.

Marlins are some of the fastest fish in the ocean. They can reach speeds of up to 50 miles per hour and one fisherman claims to have recorded a black marlin swimming 80 miles per hour. The marlin's sleek body shape that tapers on both ends is to thank for their speed.

80mph

Marlins are solitary and live alone from the time they hatch other than during mating. They migrate long distances and tend to stay near the surface where it is warm, and they can best hunt. Marlins typically hunt dense schools of fish.

FACT:
Marlins are closely related to swordfish.

FINAL WORDS OF
ENCOURAGEMENT

Isn't nature amazing? Now that you are a seasoned naturalist, you can continue to draw the world around you. Never stop exploring and asking questions!

And remember, if your drawings look different than the ones in this book, that's okay! Your drawings don't have to be perfect. The more you draw the better you will get. Not to mention it might look different because YOU drew it! There may be a million other people who have drawn this, but no one did it like you!

NATURE JOURNAL

Date: _____ / _____ / _____

Location: _____

Draw what you see:

Describe what you found:

_____

_____

_____

_____

What questions do you have?

_____

_____

_____

_____

_____

Write down three observations:
(What do you smell, hear, feel, see, etc.)

1. _____

2. _____

3. _____

🔍 TAKE A CLOSER LOOK

What details do you see when you look closer?

Grab a grownup and go explore the area around you.

What did you find? Record your observations and draw what you see!

NATURE JOURNAL

Date: /   /

Location:

Draw what you see:

Describe what you found:

What questions do you have?

_____

_____

_____

_____

_____

Write down three observations:

(What do you smell, hear, feel, see, etc.)

1. _____

2. _____

3. _____

⌕ TAKE A CLOSER LOOK

What details do you see when you look closer?

Grab a grownup and go explore the area around you.

What did you find? Record your observations and draw what you see!

NATURE JOURNAL

Date: ____ / ____ / ____

Location: _____

Draw what you see:

Describe what you found:

_____

_____

_____

_____

What questions do you have?

Write down three observations:
(What do you smell, hear, feel, see, etc.)

1.
2.
3.

TAKE A CLOSER LOOK

What details do you see when you look closer?

Grab a grownup and go explore the area around you.

What did you find? Record your observations and draw what you see!

NATURE JOURNAL

Date: /   /

Location:

Draw what you see:

Describe what you found:

What questions do you have?

_____

_____

_____

_____

_____

Write down three observations:
(What do you smell, hear, feel, see, etc.)

1. _____

2. _____

3. _____

TAKE A CLOSER LOOK

What details do you see when you look closer?

Grab a grownup and go explore the area around you.

What did you find? Record your observations and draw what you see!

NATURE JOURNAL

Date: _____ / _____ / _____

Location:

Draw what you see:

Describe what you found:

What questions do you have?

_____

_____

_____

_____

_____

Write down three observations:

(What do you smell, hear, feel, see, etc.)

1. _____

2. _____

3. _____

⌕ TAKE A CLOSER LOOK

What details do you see when you look closer?

Grab a grownup and go explore the area around you.

What did you find? Record your observations and draw what you see!

NATURE JOURNAL

Date: _____ / _____ / _____

Location: _____

Draw what you see:

Describe what you found:

_____

_____

_____

_____

What questions do you have?

_____

_____

_____

_____

_____

Write down three observations:
(What do you smell, hear, feel, see, etc.)

1. _____

2. _____

3. _____

TAKE A CLOSER LOOK

What details do you see when you look closer?

Grab a grownup and go explore the area around you.
What did you find? Record your observations and draw what you see!

NATURE JOURNAL

Date: _____ / _____ / _____

Location: _____

Draw what you see:

Describe what you found:

_____

_____

_____

_____

What questions do you have?

Write down three observations:

(What do you smell, hear, feel, see, etc.)

1.
2.
3.

TAKE A CLOSER LOOK

What details do you see when you look closer?

Grab a grownup and go explore the area around you.

What did you find? Record your observations and draw what you see!

NATURE JOURNAL

Date: _____ / _____ / _____

Location: _____

Draw what you see:

Describe what you found:

_____

_____

_____

_____

What questions do you have?

_____

_____

_____

_____

_____

Write down three observations:

(What do you smell, hear, feel, see, etc.)

1. _____

2. _____

3. _____

TAKE A CLOSER LOOK

What details do you see when you look closer?

Grab a grownup and go explore the area around you.

What did you find? Record your observations and draw what you see!

NATURE JOURNAL

Date: ____ / ____ / ____

Location: _____

Draw what you see:

Describe what you found:

_____

_____

_____

_____

What questions do you have?

Write down three observations:
(What do you smell, hear, feel, see, etc.)

1.

2.

3.

TAKE A CLOSER LOOK

What details do you see when you look closer?

Grab a grownup and go explore the area around you.
What did you find? Record your observations and draw what you see!

NATURE JOURNAL

Date: /   /

Location:

Draw what you see:

Describe what you found:

What questions do you have?

_____

_____

_____

_____

_____

Write down three observations:
(What do you smell, hear, feel, see, etc.)

1. _____

2. _____

3. _____

🔍 TAKE A CLOSER LOOK

What details do you see when you look closer?

Grab a grownup and go explore the area around you.
What did you find? Record your observations and draw what you see!

NATURE JOURNAL

Date: _____ / _____ / _____

Location: _____

Draw what you see:

Describe what you found:

_____

_____

_____

_____

What questions do you have?

_____

_____

_____

_____

_____

Write down three observations:
(What do you smell, hear, feel, see, etc.)

1. _____

2. _____

3. _____

🔍 TAKE A CLOSER LOOK

What details do you see when you look closer?

Grab a grownup and go explore the area around you.

What did you find? Record your observations and draw what you see!

NATURE JOURNAL

Date: /   /

Location:

Draw what you see:

Describe what you found:

What questions do you have?

_____

_____

_____

_____

Write down three observations:
(What do you smell, hear, feel, see, etc.)

1. _____

2. _____

3. _____

TAKE A CLOSER LOOK

What details do you see when you look closer?

Grab a grownup and go explore the area around you.

What did you find? Record your observations and draw what you see!

NATURE JOURNAL

Date: /   /

Location:

Draw what you see:

Describe what you found:

What questions do you have?

_____

_____

_____

_____

_____

Write down three observations:

(What do you smell, hear, feel, see, etc.)

1. _____

2. _____

3. _____

TAKE A CLOSER LOOK

What details do you see when you look closer?

Grab a grownup and go explore the area around you.

What did you find? Record your observations and draw what you see!

Animal Photo Credits

Stingray – JENG BO YUAN/Shutterstock.com

Angler fish – Neil Bromhall/Shutterstock.com

Flounder – IrinaK/Shutterstock.com

Damselfish – Chris Cheung/Shutterstock.com

Butterfly fish – Vladislav Gajic/Shutterstock.com

Angelfish – serg_dibrova/Shutterstock.com

Parrotfish – Miroslav Halama/Shutterstock.com

Moray eel – AdrianNunez/Shutterstock.com

Lionfish – dimakig/Shutterstock.com

Clam – Gabe Dubois/Shutterstock.com

Squid – Rui Palma/Shutterstock.com

Blue whale – Richard Carey/Adobe Stock

Portuguese man o' war – KarenHBlack/Shutterstock.com

Clown fish – thomasLENNE/Adobe Stock

Narwhal – dottedyeti/Adobe Stock

Mahi mahi – Jim/Adobe Stock

Marlin – wildestanimal/Adobe Stock

Manta ray – Tropicalens/Shutterstock.com

Tuna – lunamarina/Adobe Stock

Walrus – Danita Delimont/Shutterstock.com

Shrimp – Mati Nitibhon/Shutterstock.com

Coral – John A. Anderson/Shutterstock.com

Hammerhead shark – Matt9122/Shutterstock.com

Hermit crab – BlueBarronPhoto/Shutterstock.com

Sea turtle – Sky Cinema/Shutterstock.com

Killer whale – Tory Kallman/Shutterstock.com

Puffer fish – FtLaud/Shutterstock.com

Manatee – Greg Amptman/Shutterstock.com

Flounder – CT Johnson/Shutterstock.com

Puffin – Krasula/Shutterstock.com

Butterfly fish – gary powell/Shutterstock.com

Angel fish – Paisan1leo/Adobe Stock

Lobster – Breck P. Kent/Shutterstock.com

Clownfish – val lawless/Shutterstock.com

Seahorse – Songquan Deng/Shutterstock.com

Octopus – Mana Photo/Shutterstock.com

Sand piper – Eddie J. Rodriquez/Shutterstock.com

Pelican – Christopher Kissling/Shutterstock.com

Conch shell – Gino Santa Maria/Shutterstock.com

Sea Otter – Daniel Morales-Franchini/Shutterstock.com

Seal – Dolores M. Harvey/Shutterstock.com

Great white shark – Shane Myers Photography/Shutterstock.com

Dolphin – Tory Kallman/Shutterstock.com

Sea anemone – pkorchagina/Shutterstock.com